PRACTICAL SOLUTIONS FOR EVERYDAY WORK PROBLEMS

PRACTICAL SOLUTIONS FOR EVERYDAY WORK PROBLEMS

by Elizabeth Chesla

NEW YORK

Chesla, Elizabeth L.
    Practical Solutions for Everyday Work Problems / by Elizabeth Chesla.
    p.   cm.   —
    ISBN 1-57685-203-2
    1. Problem solving.   2. Decision making.   3. Creative ability in
business.   I. Title.   II. Series.
HD30.29.C445 1999
658.4'03—dc21   99-11368
                                                  CIP

Printed in the United States of America
9 8 7 6 5 4 3 2 1
First Edition

For Further Information
For information on LearningExpress, other LearningExpress products, or bulk
sales, please write to us at:
    LearningExpress™
    900 Broadway
    Suite 604
    New York, NY 10003

Please visit LearningExpress on the World Wide Web at *www.LearnX.com*

ISBN 1-57685-203-2

CONTENTS

INTRODUCTION

The problem is, we can't get away from problems. No matter who we are or what we do, we all have to face them. What we can control is how we handle them. We can let problems weigh us down and frighten us into inaction, or we can use problem-solving strategies to tackle even the most difficult challenges that come our way.

Effective problem solvers go places. Their ability to handle difficult situations, to somehow avoid disaster and make things right again, makes them extremely valuable in the workplace. And the benefits of their problem-solving skills aren't confined to the office alone. Effective problem solvers may not have fewer problems than the rest of us, but because they know how to handle those problems, they do tend to have less stress, more success, and more fun at home, at school, and at play.

This book is designed to help you solve problems both confidently and effectively—especially those problems that you may face on the job. If you ever feel paralyzed by problems, if you're in a position where you manage others, if you work regularly on a team, or if your job is of a "fix it" nature (for example, a customer service representative), this book is for you. You will come to know what it takes to be a confident, effective problem solver by learning how to master the steps in the problem-solving process: clearly identify the problem, determine its scope, research the problem, brainstorm effective solutions, determine the best solution, and effectively implement and present your solution to others. You'll also learn how to cultivate a problem-solving disposition, how to jump-start your creativity, and how to recognize and prevent common errors in reasoning.

In the chapters ahead, you'll learn and practice these problem-solving strategies in 20 short lessons that can be completed in about 20 minutes a day. If you read one chapter a day, Monday through Friday, and do all of the exercises carefully, you should see dramatic improvement in your ability to solve problems by the end of your month of study.

HOW TO USE THIS BOOK

Although each chapter in this book is designed to be an effective skill builder on its own, it is important that you proceed through this book in order, from Chapter 1 through Chapter 20. Like most other skills, problem-solving skills develop in layers. Each chapter in this book builds upon the ideas discussed in previous chapters, so if you don't have a thorough understanding of the concepts taught in the chapters in Section I, you won't get the full benefit of the chapters in Section II. Please be sure you thoroughly understand each chapter before moving on to the next one.

The book is divided into five sections composed of several closely related chapters. The sections are organized as follows:

Section I: Outlining the Problem
Section II: Developing a Problem-Solving Disposition
Section III: Finding a Solution
Section IV: Evaluating Your Solutions
Section V: Implementing and Presenting Your Solution

Each chapter provides exercises that allow you to practice the skills you learn throughout the book. Most of the exercises ask you to put what you learn into immediate practice by applying problem-solving strategies to both hypothetical problems and real problems you're currently facing at work. You'll find sample answers and explanations for these practice exercises to help you be sure you're on the right track. Each chapter also provides practical "Skill Building" ideas: simple problem-solving tasks you can do throughout the day or week to sharpen the skills you learn in each chapter.

THE RIGHT ATTITUDE

Like many other areas in life, when it comes to problem solving, attitude can make all the difference. If we are afraid of problems or are easily frustrated by them, we are less likely to be open to ideas and therefore less likely to find creative and effective solutions to our problems. Remember that problem-solving is a *skill* that everyone can master, and by reading this book, you've taken the first step toward becoming an effective problem solver. You will learn how to control your problems instead of letting them control you.

You can enhance your learning experience by following these suggestions:

Open up. Problem solving begins with being open to the world around you. Keep your eyes, ears, and mind open. Become an active listener. Really *look* at the people, places, and things around you. Consider ideas and possibilities that may seem strange or "wrong" to you. The more open you are, the easier it will be for you to think about problems creatively and effectively.

Stimulate your imagination. Do something creative on a regular basis—every day, if possible. Draw, paint, play music, sculpt, sing, dance. Write a story or poem. Make a collage. Decorate. Try a new recipe—or create one of your own. Stimulating your imagination will make it easier for you to find effective solutions to problems by minimizing the sense of fear that often keeps people from thinking creatively.

Cultivate your curiosity. Be like a five year old—ask about everything. Why? How? Find the answers to your questions. Why *does* thunder happen? How *does* a clock keep time?

Broaden your horizons. Try new things; gain new experiences. Go places you've never been before. Discover new worlds—at museums, parks, cultural centers. Eat at a restaurant with a cuisine you've never tried. Watch a foreign film; learn a foreign language. The broader your range of experience, the more ideas you'll have to tap into when you're brainstorming a solution for a problem. In addition, a broad range of experiences will mean that you'll be more open to new ideas and new ways of thinking about the world around you.

SECTION | I

OUTLINING THE PROBLEM

Most of us aren't trained as professional problem solvers, yet we all face countless types of problems in the workplace. The chapters in this section are designed to give you a solid understanding of just what a problem is and how to assess the scope of a problem so that you can develop the most effective solution. Specifically, you'll learn:

- What a problem is, and how problems are different from issues
- How to identify a problem
- How to break a problem down into its parts
- The difference between fact and opinion, and how this applies to problem solving
- How to gather all the facts and summarize a problem

Did you read the introduction to this book? If you didn't, please go back and read the introduction before you go on with this section.

CHAPTER | 1

JUST WHAT *IS* A PROBLEM?

There may be countless types of problems, but they all share the same basic characteristics. This chapter defines the word *problem*, explains the two-part problem structure, and distinguishes problems from *issues*.

WORDS FROM THE WISE

"The most important thing to do in solving a problem is to begin."
—*Frank Tyger*

Motivational trainers often suggest that we drop the word *problem* from our vocabulary and replace it with the word *opportunity*. In a sense, they're right—problems *are* opportunities: opportunities to channel your creative energies, to think of new ideas, to develop effective solutions. But *problem* and *opportunity* are not exactly interchangeable. After all, problems are opportunities, but opportunities are not necessarily problems.

So let's begin our study of problem solving in the workplace with a clear definition of the word *problem:*

Simply put, a problem is a situation that shouldn't be, or that should be some other way. A problem also involves some degree of difficulty; if it's easy to change *what is* to *what should be,* it's not really a problem. When you do have a problem, *how* you change the situation from what is to what should be is the *solution.*

> **Problem**: An undesirable situation that is difficult to change.
>
> **Solution**: The mechanism of change.

This definition of problem helps us distinguish between things that really aren't problems and things that are. For example, if you're on your way to a meeting and you get stuck in traffic, that's certainly an undesirable situation, but you may not have a problem. If you have a cell phone and can let the right people know that you'll be late, you may still be stuck, but you've changed the situation (postponed the meeting) with a simple phone call. However, if the folks you're meeting with can't wait for you, or if you don't have a phone to call from, then you probably do have a problem—you haven't been able to change the undesirable situation.

Because problems require solutions, they're best expressed in a two-part structure:

1. A statement that explains the current problematic situation.
2. A question that expresses the desired situation or goal.

Part two, the question that expresses the desired situation or goal, is our guide for developing an effective solution. Therefore, the desired goal is usually best expressed as a question using the question word *how.* For example:

1. **Current situation:** I'm not happy at my job.

   Desired situation: How can I find a job that is less stressful and more rewarding?

2. **Current situation:** I love my job but I'm barely able to pay the bills.

   Desired situation: *How* can I earn enough money to make ends meet?

3. **Current situation:** Johnson needs the plans by tomorrow at 7 a.m.

   Desired situation: *How* can we get the plans finished in time?

Each of these examples clearly states the problem—the undesirable situation that *is*—and then asks a question that spells out a specific goal—the situation that *should be.*

Practice:

List several problems you've dealt with recently or are dealing with currently. Use the two-part problem structure to state your problems.

1. Current situation:

   Desired situation:

2. Current situation:

   Desired situation:

3. Current situation:

   Desired situation:

Answers:

Answers will vary. Here are some possibilities:

1. **Current situation:** I lost my beeper.

   Desired situation: How can people get in touch with me until I get a replacement?

2. **Current situation:** I have two reports due tomorrow and haven't started either one.

   Desired situation: How can I get them done (and done well) on time?

3. **Current situation:** I requested Thursday night off for my daughter's recital, but the recital is on Wednesday, not Thursday.

Desired situation: How can I get Wednesday night off instead?

THE DIFFERENCE BETWEEN PROBLEMS AND ISSUES

A common pitfall in problem solving is to confuse *problems* and *issues*. An issue is a point in question, an item of controversy. When it comes to issues, we may be seeking *answers* (whether we should believe something or accept something as right or true), but we are not seeking a *solution* (a plan to get the desired results).

Issue: A point in question or item of controversy.

We can express issues in questions as well, but, since we're not seeking a *solution*, the question word should illicit a "yes" or "no" response, as in the following examples:

- *Should* there be random drug testing in the workplace?
- *Should* there be a no-smoking policy in the office?
- *Is* an employee's company email private property or company property?
- *Do* employers have the right to curtail employees' activities outside of the workplace?

The "yes" or "no," of course, should only be arrived at after much debate. Remember, an issue is a point in dispute, so there are undoubtedly many sides to consider before determining your position on the issue.

Practice:
List several issues that are important to you. Make sure at least two of those issues are work related.

1.

2.

3.

4.

Answers:

Answers will vary. Here are some possibilities:

1. Are women more effective managers than men?

2. Should large corporations be required to provide child care on the premises?

3. Should tax breaks be used as incentives to get companies to comply with environmental protection laws?

Kinds of Problems

There are, of course, many different kinds of problems. Problems can be individual or personal, or they can be collective or societal. They can involve finances, relationships, education, communication, politics, values—just about anything. Problems of all types can be found in the workplace. Here are just a few examples:

1. **Current situation:** We have $2,000 to develop and print a company brochure.

   Desired situation: How can we accomplish this task on such a low budget?

2. **Current situation:** Johnson misunderstood what I said and thinks that I disagree with his position.

   Desired situation: How can I convince him that I support his position?

3. **Current situation:** There is bound to be a lot of resistance to my proposal for a four-day work week.

   Desired situation: How can I get support for this proposal?

4. **Current situation:** My work area is cluttered and I can never find anything.

   Desired situation: How can I arrange this workspace so that I can find the information I need quickly and easily?

5. **Current situation:** Joe has asked me to lie about an incident but I believe that he should take responsibility for what happened.

   Desired situation: How do I keep Joe's friendship without compromising my beliefs?

Because there are so many types of problems in the workplace, it may be helpful to divide them into three categories:

Personal: Problems that primarily affect you as a person.

Professional: Problems that primarily affect you as an employee.

Corporate: Problems that primarily affect the company as a whole.

In the previous examples, problem 1 is corporate; 2, 3, and 4 are professional; and 5 is personal.

Of course, because you are an employee, most problems that affect you personally or professionally will also affect the corporation to some degree, and vice versa. These categories do not have clear-cut boundaries; they're simply one way to help us organize and prioritize our problems.

Practice:

List at least one personal, professional, and corporate problem you have faced on the job in your last year of work. Be sure to use the two-part problem structure.

1.

2.

3.

Answers:

Answers will vary. Here are some possibilities:

1. *Personal:*

   Current situation: The new snack machine has been placed right outside my office door.

   Desired situation: How can I prevent myself from snacking all day long?

2. *Professional:*

   Current situation: The co-worker next to me talks all day long and I can't get any work done.

   Desired situation: How can I get him to stop talking so I can be more productive?

3. *Corporate:*

Current situation: There has been an increase in customer service complaints.

Desired situation: How can we reduce—if not eliminate—customer complaints?

 ## WORDS FROM THE WISE

"All problems become smaller if you don't dodge them but confront them."
—*William F. Halsey*

In Short

Problems are undesirable situations that are difficult to change. They are best expressed in a two-part problem statement that describes the current situation and asks *how* a specific, desired goal can be reached. The *solution* is the mechanism employed to change the current situation to the desired situation. Problems are different from *issues*, which are points of contention or controversy. Issues are best expressed with question words like *is*, *does*, or *should*.

Skill Building Until Next Time

1. Listen to how people talk about problems. What attitude toward problem solving do their words convey? Do they tend to confuse problems with issues?
2. Consider the problems you listed in this chapter and others that are affecting you now and in the recent past. How would you categorize them? Use the categories described in this chapter, or come up with categories that seem most appropriate for you. Place your problems in those categories. Do your problems seem to fall into one category more than others? Why might this be?

CHAPTER | 2

IDENTIFYING THE PROBLEM, PART I: THE CURRENT SITUATION

Successful problem solving depends upon a clearly identified problem. This chapter explains how to identify and express the current situation so you can develop an effective solution.

It's one thing to know that there's a problem. It's another thing altogether to be able to identify exactly what the problem is.

Unfortunately, all too often we fail to solve our problems because we come up with a solution for the *wrong problem*. That is, we make a critical mistake in the first step of the problem-solving process: identifying the problem.

Identifying the problem seems like such an obvious step that you might be wondering why we even need a chapter on it. After all, how can you solve a problem if you don't know what the problem is? But while it may be an obvious step, it's not necessarily an *easy* step. And that's why we've dedicated not just one but two chapters to this topic—one for each part of the problem statement.

IDENTIFYING THE EXISTING SITUATION

A problem is a problem precisely because the *current situation* (A) is not *what you would like it to be* (B). To move from point A to point B, however, you need to be sure you *are* at point A. That is, you need to accurately identify what it is about the current situation that is problematic. Otherwise, your problem-solving efforts may be in vain. If you think you're going from point A to point B, but you weren't at A to begin with, then whatever solution you come up with is likely to be off base. It's like getting directions to drive from Philadelphia to Memphis, but you're not really in Philadelphia—you're in Chicago.

When people incorrectly identify the existing problem, it's often because they do not look at the situation objectively. That is, they allow their emotions and desires to cloud their judgment, and, as a result, they are unable to see the situation as it really is. Or perhaps they know what the situation is, but are unable to express it in anything but a biased way. Problems are also incorrectly identified when the problem solver lacks focus. That is, the problem-solver may be trying to solve a problem that is too big (world hunger, for example) instead of focusing on a more immediate and solvable problem (like hunger in his or her own neighborhood).

The key to accurately stating the existing problem, then, is twofold:

1. Make sure your problem statement is a statement of *fact*, not opinion; and

2. Make sure your problem statement is *manageable.*

WORDS FROM THE WISE

"Before it can be solved, a problem must be clearly stated and defined."
—*William Feather*

Fact vs. Opinion
Before we go any further let's clarify the difference between *fact* and *opinion:*

Facts are:

- Things *known* for certain to have happened
- Things *known* for certain to be true
- Things *known* for certain to exist

Opinions, on the other hand, are:

- Things *believed* to have happened
- Things *believed* to be true
- Things *believed* to exist

Essentially, the difference between fact and opinion is the difference between *believing* and *knowing*. Opinions may be *based* on facts, but they are still what we *think*, not what we *know*. Opinions are debatable; facts usually are not. A good test for whether something is a fact or opinion is to ask yourself, "Can this statement be debated? Is this known for certain to be true?" If you can answer *yes* to the first question, you have an opinion; if you answer *yes* to the second, you have a fact.

FACT	OPINION
Something **known** for certain to have happened, to be true, or to exist.	Something **believed** to have happened, to be true, or to exist.
Not debatable.	Debatable.

Practice:

Read the following statements carefully. Which of the following are facts? Opinions? Write an F in the blank if it is a fact and an O if it is an opinion.

_____ 1. Tyler Products is having a record year.

_____ 2. Tyler Products has an outstanding training program and great benefits.

_____ 3. Tyler employees enjoy full tuition reimbursement for any college course, regardless of whether or not it applies to a degree.

_____ 4. If more companies offered Tyler's salary and benefits, there'd be fewer strikes.

Answers:

1-F; 2-O; 3-F; 4-O

PROBLEMATIC PROBLEM STATEMENTS

When your problem statements are not factual, you run the risk of derailing your entire problem-solving process. After all, your goal is based on your description of the problem, and your solution is based on your goal. For example, imagine that you have difficulties with one of your co-workers, Glenn. Your boss created work teams, and you have been assigned to group B—and so has Glenn. Now, look at the following problem statements:

1. **Current situation:** I've been placed on a project team with Glenn.

   Desired situation: How can I minimize my interactions with Glenn without jeopardizing the project or my job?

2. **Current situation:** Glen is a creep.

   Desired situation: How can I avoid working with him?

3. **Current situation:** I need to be on a different team.

   Desired situation: How can I get out of this group?

Problem statement #1, of course, is the most effective of the three. Why? Partly because its description of the current situation is fact, simple and straight-forward. In the second example, the current situation is clearly expressing an opinion—and not a particularly constructive one at that. Its lack of objectivity will lead to a misdirected goal and therefore a solution to the wrong problem. You don't need to know how to avoid working with Glenn; that won't change the current situation.

The third problem statement is ineffective because it, too, lacks objectivity. It not only expresses an opinion, it also suggests a solution. A problem statement that suggests a solution has several negative effects. First, your goal will be misdirected. Second, suggesting a solution in your problem statement will severely limit your ability to brainstorm for effective solutions.

Practice:

Are any problem statements below that are not objective facts? If so, rewrite them so they are more effective.

1. My job is boring.

2. We need a new heating system.

3. I've been transferred to the uptown office.

Answers:

1. This is an opinion. A better problem statement would be: *I'm often bored at work.*

2. This suggests a solution. A better problem statement would be: *Our current heating system breaks down every week.*

3. This is an objective statement of fact.

MANAGEABLE PROBLEM STATEMENTS

Your profits are plummeting, and you suspect it has something to do with the recent economic recession. So you express your problem as follows:

Current situation: The economy is in a recession.

Now, the recession may indeed be a problem —for you, for your company, for the whole country. But if you start with this broad fact as your problem statement, two things will likely result: 1) your problem will get worse, not better; and 2) you'll end up being very, very frustrated. Why?

Effective problem solvers know that problem statements must not only be *facts*; they must also be *focused*. Focusing the problem statement makes it *manageable*. We may want to correct the economic downturn, end world hunger, bring about world peace—but these problems are far too large for us to tackle successfully. Instead, focusing on a piece of the larger problem— something within our own *sphere of influence*—enables us to effectively address and resolve the problem. Of course, throughout the problem-solving process we should keep in mind the "big picture," but remember that the effects of what you do can only reach so far. Your problem statement, then, should address a specific, focused problem that *you can do something about.*

Practice:

Identify and revise any problem statements that seem unfocused or unmanageable for the person in that position.

1. Angelo Fernandez, bank teller: Customers want more options for investing.

2. Ellen Yin, legal secretary: I haven't finished typing the transcripts needed for this afternoon's deposition.

3. Madeline Walters, administrative assistant: My co-worker doesn't know Excel and I end up doing a lot of his work.

4. Lewis Johnson, computer store cashier: The national office raised prices again.

Answers:

1. This problem statement is unmanageable. As a bank teller, Fernandez may be able to present his ideas or opinions to upper management, but he has no real influence over what investment options the bank will offer.

2. This problem statement is focused and manageable.

3. This problem statement is also focused and manageable.

4. This problem statement is unmanageable. As a cashier, Johnson has no influence on the prices of equipment for sale in the store.

In Short

The first step in effective problem solving is to clearly identify and express the current undesirable situation. In order to yield a solution, the problem statement must be a fact (something that is known for sure to be true); it should not express opinion or suggest a solution. Problem statements must also be manageable—focused enough to express a problem within the problem solver's sphere of influence.

Skill Building Until Next Time

1. Listen carefully to how people express their problems. Do they use opinion to describe the current situation? Suggest solutions? Are their problem statements manageable, or do they lack focus?
2. Go back to Chapter 1 and look at the problems you listed in the first practice exercise. Do you need to revise the way you described the current situations?

CHAPTER | 3

IDENTIFYING THE PROBLEM, PART II: THE DESIRED STATE OR GOAL

O nce you've clearly identified the problem, you need to articulate the desired situation. This chapter shows you how to complete your problem statement by developing a problem-solving goal that is specific and realistic.

 ### WORDS FROM THE WISE

"Give me a stock clerk with a goal and I will give you a man who will make history. Give me a man without a goal, and I will give you a stock clerk."

—*J.C. Penney*

Have you ever gone to the grocery store when you were very hungry but didn't know what you wanted to eat? Did you find yourself wandering aimlessly aisle after aisle, looking for that unknown food that would satisfy you—and all the while your problem (your hunger) grew more and more unbearable?

Now compare that to a trip to the grocery store when you know exactly what you want to eat. You have a list. You head straight to the aisles that contain your items, and your trip is quick and effective. The difference between these two situations is clear: In the first instance, you set out to solve a problem, but you only articulated the *problem*. In the second instance, you identified both the problem *and* a specific *goal*.

The first step in successful problem solving is to identify the current, problematic situation. The second step is to identify the *desired* state or situation—that is, to clearly articulate your problem-solving goal.

A clearly articulated goal is essential to reaching an effective solution. You can find dozens of ways to change the situation, but not all of those ways will get you the kind of change you desire. In other words, it's not enough to know that you want to change the current situation. For effective problem solving, you need to know exactly what you want to change the current situation *to*. Otherwise, it'd be like knowing you're in Memphis and knowing that you need to be someplace else, but not knowing *where* that place is. If you don't know your destination, how can you determine how to get there? All the maps in the world won't do you any good unless you know where you want to go.

A clearly defined goal, then, enables you to focus your problem-solving energies on generating a solution that will get you exactly where you want to go—when you want to get there.

GOAL SETTING

A goal, of course, is something you are trying to reach or achieve. You're using this book, for example, because you have a specific goal: to become a more effective problem solver.

Goal: Something you are trying to reach or achieve.

Whether you're working on a problem statement or outlining career or personal goals, there are four guidelines for effective goal setting that you should follow:

1. Make sure your goals are *specific.*

2. Make sure your goals are *measurable.*

3. Make sure your goals are *ambitious.*

4. Make sure your goals are *realistic.*

Specific and Measurable

Take a look at the following problem statement:

> **Current situation:** I don't know anything about computers.
>
> **Desired situation:** How can I learn about computers?

What's wrong with this problem statement? The way the current situation is expressed is fine—it's a statement of fact, and it's focused enough to be solvable. But the way the desired situation is expressed is problematic. If you want to learn about computers, you need to be much more specific about *what* you need to learn. Otherwise, how can you determine the best way to learn that information? With such a general question, we'd be hard pressed to come up with an effective solution; different information about computers can be learned in many different ways. A much more specific, and, therefore, much more effective, expression of the goal would look like this:

> **Desired situation:** How can I learn how to do word processing and basic document design in Microsoft Word?

Now we can work toward a solution because we know specific changes that need to be made to the current situation. That is, we know exactly what we need to learn.

Here's another example—in Chapter 1, we presented the following problem statement:

Current situation: I'm not happy at my job.

Desired situation: How can I find a job that is less stressful and more rewarding?

Notice how this desired situation specifies the kind of change desired—a job that is *less stressful* and *more rewarding*. This helps us better focus our efforts as we search for a solution.

In addition to being specific, your goal should also be *measurable*. For example, look at the following problem statement:

Current situation: Profits are down.

Desired situation: How can we increase profits?

Unless we know by *how much* we want to increase profits, we aren't going to come up with the most effective or appropriate solution. That's because the best solution will vary according to the profit-growth goals. The solution for increasing profits by 5%, for example, will be *very* different from the solution for increasing profits by 50%. Thus, the more specific we are in our goal statement about *what* we want changed, and *how much* or *to what degree* we want it changed, the easier it will be to develop an effective solution.

Practice:

Are the desired situations in the following problem statements specific and measurable? If not, revise them so they're more effective.

1. **Current situation:** The computer system is down.

   Desired situation: How can I get any work done?

2. **Current situation:** I still don't have the data I need to complete my report, which is due today.

   Desired situation: How can I complete my report without that data?

3. **Current situation:** The customer refuses to pay the full amount because he insists we overcharged him.

   Desired situation: How can I get him to pay?

Answers:

1. This goal needs to be revised. A better question would be: *How can I type up my reports and update my files without my computer?*

2. This question is specific and measurable.

3. This question could be more specific. A better question would be: *How can I get him to pay the full amount in this billing period?*

WORDS FROM THE WISE

"If you don't know where you are going, every road will get you nowhere."
—*Henry Kissinger*

Ambitious but Realistic

Imagine for a moment that you want to save money to buy a new car. You open a savings account and establish the following goal:

Desired situation: I'll save at least $5 each week.

Of course, every penny counts, but $5 a week adds up to just $110 a year—not a tremendous amount, and certainly not enough for a down payment on a new automobile. When you realize this, you revise your goal to the following:

Desired situation: I'll save at least $200 each week.

At this rate you'll have $10,400 in just one year—down payment and then some. But $200 a week is rather steep—that's $800 a month. Whereas the first goal was not ambitious enough, the second is probably too ambitious. Unless you earn a very high salary or have virtually no bills, you're probably setting yourself up for failure because it's not a goal that you'll be able to meet. It's simply not realistic.

When you're developing your problem-solving goal, you should find a healthy compromise: make the goal a challenge, but a challenge that is attainable. That is, aim high, but not so high that you'll never be able to reach your goal.

For example, let's say you want to earn a college degree, but you can only attend school part-time. You know it's probably unrealistic to say "I'd like to have my degree in four years" if you can only take classes part-time. But it's not much of a challenge to say "How can I earn my degree in the next twenty years?" Compromise by stating a goal that is both challenging and reasonable, like the following:

Desired situation: How can I earn my bachelor's degree in the next six years or less?

Notice that this goal is both specific and measurable.

As you consider your goal, remember that people tend to live up to expectations. If you tell your production team you want to increase output by 1%, for example, you'll probably get an increase of exactly that—1%. But by asking for an increase of 10%, you suggest that you believe your team can achieve that goal. While they may only achieve an increase of 8%, that's still 7% higher than 1%. On the other hand, if you set your goal too high and tell your team you want an increase of 50%, your team might not make any effort at all because they know it's not possible.

Practice:

Are the desired situations in the following problem statements ambitious but realistic? If not, revise them so that they are.

1. **Current situation:** I'm not happy with my current job.

   Desired situation: How can I get a new job by next week?

2. **Current situation:** I'm earning a C in my history class, and I need a B to get tuition reimbursement.

   Desired situation: How can I get my average up to an A?

3. **Current situation:** My new job requires a lot of data entry but I don't know how to type.

   Desired situation: How can I learn to type in the next year?

Answers:

1. If you're looking for *any* job, then a week is probably realistic. The problem is that this question doesn't specify what kind of job. Assuming that you're searching for the same kind of job you have now, this goal is probably too ambitious to be realistic. Conducting an effective job search usually takes three months or more.

2. This may be a little too ambitious to be realistic. You're asking to move your grade from the 70s to the 90s. How realistic it is depends upon two things—how high or low your C is, and how far you are into the semester (that is, how much time you have to improve your average). Obviously, the earlier it is in the semester and the higher your C, the more realistic.

3. This goal is certainly realistic, but it's not very ambitious. A month would be more appropriate.

In Short

To be effective, problem statements not only need a clearly expressed problem, they also need a clearly defined goal. Your desired situation should express a *specific, measurable, ambitious,* and *realistic* goal. This will enable you to develop a solution that takes you from point A (the current situation) to point B (the desired situation) effectively.

Skill Building Until Next Time

1. Go back to Chapter 1 and look at the problems you listed in the first practice exercise. Should any of your desired situations be revised?

2. Consider several problems you've heard others discuss recently. How would you express the current situation? The desired situation?

CHAPTER | 4

BREAKING THE PROBLEM INTO ITS PARTS

W e're often frightened by problems because they seem too big to handle. This chapter shows you how to determine the scope of a problem and make it manageable by breaking it down into its parts.

You know your starting point (the problem) and your destination (your goal). But before you begin to plan your trip (your solution) there are two important steps to take: (1) determine the scope of the problem and (2) research and summarize the problem. We'll deal with the first step in this lesson and the second step in Chapter 5.

Analyzing the current situation and breaking it down into its parts enables you to determine the scope of the problem (how big it is, how many aspects are involved) and make it manageable (by dealing with small pieces of the problem one at a time). As a result, you can more easily come up with a systematic and appropriate solution.

DETERMINING THE SCOPE OF THE PROBLEM

The best way to determine the scope of the problem is to ask questions based on the problem statement. For example, look at the following problem statement:

Current situation: Customers are complaining that their products take more than six weeks to be delivered.

Desired situation: To have products in customers' hands in three weeks or less.

To begin, ask a series of *who, what, when, where, why,* and *how* questions based on the current situation. List as many questions as possible. Below is a list of questions for the problem above. Note that the overarching question here is the first one:

- *Why are the products taking so long to be delivered?*
- What products are being complained about? (Is it all products, or just a certain few?)
- When did we start receiving complaints?
- How long after a customer places an order is it shipped?
- Where do orders go when they come in?
- How much is charged for shipping and handling?
- What exactly happens to an order once it is placed? What are the steps in the order-fulfillment process?
- How are products shipped?
- Who handles the orders once they are placed?
- Who handles the shipping?

Once we develop a list of questions, we can clearly see the scope of the problem, which includes not just the delivering of the product, but how the order is processed and everything in between. To develop an effective solution to this problem, we need to answer these and other questions that may arise in our investigation.

WORDS FROM THE WISE

"'Why' and 'How' are words so important that they cannot be too often used."

—*Napoleon Bonaparte*

Practice:

List questions to determine the scope of the following problem:

Current situation: I have to ask current customers basic information because the customer information files are almost always incomplete.

Desired situation: How can we ensure that customer information files are complete?

Questions:

Answers:

Answers will vary. Here are some possibilities:

- How is a customer file created?
- Who creates it?
- Where are files kept?
- Is the information in a central database?
- How is information updated?
- What information is needed from a customer for the average transaction?
- How can that information be made available without access to the customer's file?

As you can see, this questioning process will usually generate a fairly extensive list of questions. Depending upon the circumstances, you may not have time to answer them all. More importantly, you may not *need* to answer them all. To maximize your time as you prepare to solve your problem, take these important steps before you begin your research:

1. Eliminate any questions that are irrelevant.
2. Cluster questions around related issues.
3. Prioritize the questions by determining the order in which they need to be answered.

DETERMINING RELEVANCE

Once you've developed a list of questions about the problem, it's important that you make sure each question is *relevant* to that problem. That is, each question should be clearly related to the matter at hand.

It's often obvious when something *isn't* relevant. Whether you like your pizza plain or with pepperoni, for example, clearly has nothing to do with this shipping problem. But the question of how much is charged for shipping and handling *might* be relevant. It depends upon whether the cost of shipping and handling determines how the products are shipped.

One thing to keep in mind is that personal preferences are often brought in as issues when they shouldn't be. For example, you may like certain colleagues better than others, but that doesn't mean the people you like are more believable than the others. In other words, your friendship with one person or another (or lack thereof) should not be relevant to the situation. (We'll talk more about this kind of bias in a later lesson.)

For the shipping problem, then, we might determine the following:

- Who is doing the complaining? *Irrelevant.*

- Who handles the orders once they are placed? *Relevant.*

- What computer program is used to track orders? *Might be relevant.*

Practice:
Look at the list of questions you developed in the previous exercise. Cross out any questions that are irrelevant. Put a question mark next to questions whose relevance is uncertain.

GROUPING QUESTIONS

Once you've eliminated any irrelevant questions, the next step is to cluster the remaining questions into groups of related issues. For example, in our shipping problem, the questions can be grouped as follows:

- Questions about the complaints

- Questions about order receipt and processing

- Questions about order fulfillment

- Questions about order shipping

Because answers to related questions can often be found in the same place, lumping the questions together like this makes it easier to find the answers you'll need to develop an effective solution. Grouping the questions will also help save time by enabling you to find a series of answers in one step instead of several.

Practice:
Group the questions you listed for the first practice exercise into related categories. Give each category an appropriate title.

PRIORITIZING QUESTIONS

When you have a list of things to do, to make the most of your time and effort, you usually prioritize them—rank them in order of importance or chronology (the order in which they must take place). The same principle applies in problem solving. Because some questions are clearly more important than others, and because certain questions must be answered before others can be addressed, it's essential to rank the questions in the order in which they need to be answered. What questions (or groups of questions) need to be addressed first? Second? Third? For example, we might organize the questions about the shipping problem as follows:

- Why are the products taking so long to be delivered?
- What products are being complained about? (Is it all products, or just a certain few?)
- When did we start receiving complaints?
- Where do orders go when they come in?
- What exactly happens to an order once it is placed? What are the steps in the order-fulfillment process?
- How long after a customer places an order is it shipped?
- How are products shipped?
- Who handles the shipping?
- How much is charged for shipping and handling?

The first thing we must do is find out more information about the complaints, then the order processing, order fulfillment, and finally order shipment.

Practice:
Prioritize the questions you grouped in the previous practice exercise.

In Short

We can make problems more manageable—and our solutions more effective—by breaking them down into parts. First, ask as many *who, what, when, where, why,* and *how* questions as possible about the current situation. Eliminate any irrelevant questions, and then cluster the remaining questions into groups of related questions. Finally, prioritize those questions so that you can find the most pertinent information right away.

Skill Building Until Next Time

1. Consider a problem you are currently facing. Formulate a problem statement, and then ask questions to determine the scope of the problem.
2. Consider a problem you faced recently. Did you break it into its parts and prioritize them? If not, how would your solution have been different if you had?

CHAPTER | 5

GATHERING THE FACTS AND SUMMARIZING THE PROBLEM

Just as a detective needs to find the facts regarding the crime in order to solve it, problem solvers need to find the facts behind the current situation in order to change it. This chapter provides several strategies for researching the problem and preparing for the next step: finding a solution.

WORDS FROM THE WISE

"It's so much easier to suggest solutions when you don't know too much about the problem."
—*Malcolm Forbes*

Customers are complaining about having to wait six weeks for their products. Your goal is to change the situation so that the products are delivered within two weeks. After some thought, you decide that the problem must lie with the shipping company, and you decide to pay your shipping company higher rates to give your packages priority. Problem solved. Right?

Well, maybe—but probably not. In fact, you may end up creating more problems rather than solving this one. Why? Because you neglected a crucial step in the problem-solving process: gathering the facts and summarizing the problem.

Maybe the reason the products take so long to be delivered is because the person who normally handles product orders quit, and the department hasn't yet found a replacement. As a result, all orders are backlogged. In this case, paying your shipping company extra isn't going to make much of a difference in when your customers receive their products—but it will make a big difference in your bank account.

Before you begin brainstorming a solution, then, it's crucial that you do your homework and find the answers to all of those questions you ask when breaking the problem into its parts. As you do your research, keep the following strategies in mind:

1. Keep accurate records.

2. Consider levels of causation.

3. Keep asking questions.

KEEP ACCURATE RECORDS

As you search for answers to your questions, be sure to accurately record those answers. Problems in the workplace tend to be complicated, and the more people there are involved, the more complicated they will be. Accurate notes will give you a paper trail of the information you've already found, so needless double-checking won't have to happen.

CONSIDER LEVELS OF CAUSATION

The key question you ask as you brainstorm about the scope of a problem is usually *why*. In the example of the shipping problem, the overarching question is, "Why are the products taking so long to be delivered?" As you conduct your research and look for answers to your questions, what you're really doing is looking for the *cause* of the problem. But don't make the mistake of assuming that there's only one cause. There may, in fact, be a chain of causation involving multiple causes.

Chain of causation. This simply means that there was a series of cause and effect relationships that led to the current situation. (C caused D, but B caused C, and A caused B; that is, A→B→C→D.) For example, the delay in shipping may be caused by the fact that Kathleen, the woman who used to process the orders, quit and no one has been hired to replace her. The fact that no one has been hired to replace Kathleen, however, has, in turn, been caused by something else: a hiring freeze. And the hiring freeze has been caused by a downturn in sales.

Keep in mind, though, that while it's important to look for a chain of causation, it can be unfruitful to follow the chain of causation too far. You'll need to use your judgement about how far back in the chain you should go. There are two questions that can help you make that judgement:

1. Is this cause still in my sphere of influence?

2. Is this cause still relevant?

If you can do something about the hiring freeze, for example—if you think the situation is critical enough that you could lobby for an exception to the hiring freeze—then that's not too far back in the chain. If, however, your position, or the financial situation of the company, limits your (or someone you can recruit to fight on your behalf) influence on the hiring freeze, then it is best to stop at the fact that no one has been hired to replace the order processing clerk. You can consider this as the main cause and use this information to determine your solution.

Multiple causes. When two or more factors work together to cause an event, you have multiple causes (A and B together cause C). These causes can be either *sufficient* or *necessary*. If A sometimes causes C, A is considered a *sufficient* cause. But if C cannot happen without A, then A is considered a *necessary* cause. For example, the hiring freeze is *sufficient* to cause the vacancy to remain unfilled. But it's not a necessary cause; there are other factors that might cause such a position remain vacant. However, a decision by the Board of Directors to enact a hiring freeze is a *necessary* cause of the freeze—the freeze couldn't happen without it.

Notice that the downturn in sales *contributed* to this cause, so that what we have here is a combination of both a chain of causation and multiple causes. Because sales went down, the Board voted in a hiring freeze; meanwhile the order processing clerk quit; and as a result the position remains vacant. We might represent the situation visually as follows:

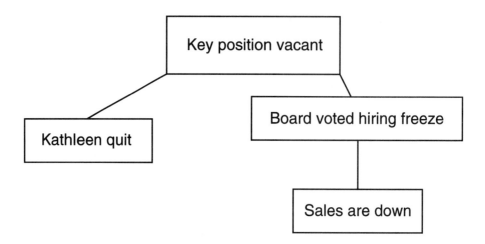

KEEP ASKING QUESTIONS

The most effective solutions are developed by the most diligent problem solvers—those who, like children, keep asking questions. Let's continue to examine the shipping problem, for example. Imagine we stopped once we found all of the answers to the questions we'd brainstormed. We might get lucky and develop an effective solution, but there's a good chance our solution would be flawed. Why? Because there are other questions that arise in every research project, and problem solving is no exception.

What other questions could we ask about this shipping problem? Well, for one thing we need to ask why Kathleen, the order processing clerk, quit. Maybe the reason has nothing to do with our problem—perhaps she was on maternity leave and decided to leave work permanently. Maybe she moved out-of-state. Maybe the reason doesn't matter. But maybe it does. Maybe she quit because she was frustrated with being the only one processing all the orders. Maybe she quit because her colleagues were prejudiced or harassed her. Maybe she quit because she was bored and there were no rewards for her in that position. All of these possibilities are relevant, and knowing which is really the case is crucial to developing an effective solution—because whatever caused Kathleen to quit may have to be addressed in order to effectively solve the problem.

Practice:
If you learned that Kathleen had quit because she felt frustrated and overworked, what other questions would you ask?

Answers:
Answers will vary. Here are some questions you might consider:

1. What were Kathleen's duties?

2. What duties took up most of her time?

3. What might someone else have been able to do to help her?

4. What was Kathleen hired to do versus what did she really do?

5. How much did she get paid?

SUMMARIZING THE PROBLEM

Once you've answered your questions and gathered all the relevant facts, it's time to summarize the problem so that you can begin working on your solution. To summarize, simply restate the current situation and the desired solution, and then list the key facts that you discovered in your research. For example:

Current situation: Customers are complaining that their products take more than six weeks to be delivered.

Desired situation: To have products in customers' hands in three weeks or less.

Key facts:

- Complaints began a month after the order processing clerk quit.
- Clerk quit because she was overworked (handled over 50 orders a day).
- Her position is still vacant.
- Orders are now handled by office manager, who can only work on orders one day a week.
- Office manager and assistant call inventory to send product to office.
- Assistant places product in box and applies labels.
- Assistant gives box to mailroom clerk, who then ships via 1st class mail.

Notice that we listed only the key information—answers to the most important questions and the information that best reveals the cause of the problem.

Practice:

Summarize the key facts for the problem below reprinted from Chapter 4 by making up answers to the questions you asked about the problem. Your questions are on page 39 in Chapter 4.

Current situation: I have to ask current customers basic information because the customer information files are almost always incomplete.

Desired situation: How can we ensure that customer information files are complete?

Key facts:

WORDS FROM THE WISE

"Get the facts, or the facts will get you. And when you get 'em, get 'em right, or they will get you wrong."
—*Thomas Fuller*

In Short

To effectively solve our problems, the questions that we ask to determine the scope of the problem must be answered. As you conduct your research, be sure to keep accurate records. Consider chains of causation as far back as your sphere of influence reaches, and consider multiple causes. As you find answers, ask more questions. Then summarize your problem by restating the current situation, the desired situation, and the key facts. You're now ready to brainstorm for a solution.

Skill Building Until Next Time

1. Gather the facts for a problem you are currently facing.
2. Imagine that a problem similar to the shipping problem were affecting your company. Do you know where you'd find the answers to your questions? How well do you know your company? Who is in charge of what information? What are the various policies and procedures?

SECTION | II

DEVELOPING A PROBLEM-SOLVING DISPOSITION

Someone who seems to be a "natural" at problem solving wasn't necessarily born with the ability to solve problems effectively. After all, problem solving is a skill that has to be learned. What makes a person a natural is that he or she has a disposition that makes problem solving easier. But you don't have to be born with such a disposition. With a little practice, you can develop the characteristics that will help make problem solving second nature for you. These characteristics include:

- A healthy attitude toward problems and problem solving
- A knowledge of the conditions in which you are most creative and productive
- An active sense of curiosity
- An ability to see things from different points of view
- A ready imagination and capacity for creativity

CHAPTER | 6

ATMOSPHERE AND ATTITUDE

How you feel about problems can make all the difference in how effective you are in solving them. This chapter explains how to approach problems with the right attitude and how to optimize your mental and physical state.

When confronted with a problem, you typically:

 a. Run and hide.

 b. Blame it on someone else.

 c. Say it's not your problem; let someone else fix it.

 d. Close your eyes and hope it goes away.

 e. Shake your head and say, "Why me?"

As negative as each if these responses may be, we often react to problems with fear, anger, frustration, or denial. The result? We make our problems worse and sometimes create other problems as well.

How we approach problems and the problem-solving process has a tremendous impact on our ability to find a successful solution. Successful problem solvers face problems with the right attitude and conduct the problem-solving process in an atmosphere that encourages their success.

WORDS FROM THE WISE

"For success, attitude is equally as important as ability."
—*Harry F. Banks*

THE RIGHT ATTITUDE

How much does attitude affect us? More than most people realize. Attitude works in our brains much like a program in a computer. That is, a negative attitude predisposes us to expect a negative experience, and, therefore, we exude negative energy. The result? We usually *do* have a negative experience. When this happens in the problem-solving process, we shut down our creative channels, blocking ideas that we might have come up with if only we'd had the right attitude.

To understand the importance of attitude, think back to a time when you had a negative attitude about something. What kind of negative thoughts influenced your experience? Were you negative about trying something new, for example? Did you say to yourself, "I can't do that!" If you said it enough, believed it was true, then you probably couldn't do it—not because you weren't capable, but because you wouldn't allow yourself to succeed. Your attitude made it a negative experience.

A positive attitude, on the other hand, opens us up, prepares us to expect good things, frees our creative energies, and leads us to success.

To help you develop the right attitude toward problem solving, we suggest the following:

Face reality. Hiding from a problem or denying that it exists will only make it worse. Problems usually don't just go away; they stick around until someone, somehow, comes up with a solution. So acknowledge the problem, and acknowledge your power to address it. You don't have to think of yourself as a super-hero, solving every problem under the sun. But do accept the fact that problems are a part of life, and you are becoming a capable and effective problem solver.

Embrace challenges. Remember, problems are opportunities. Think of each situation as a chance to develop your problem-solving skills, your analytical abilities, and your creativity. Problems are also a chance to learn from your mistakes. Don't shy away from a problem or other opportunity because you are afraid to fail. *Failure is essential for success.* Babe Ruth is world-famous for his home runs, but did you know he also struck out thousands of times? (Imagine if he focused on those strikeouts instead of his home runs!) He didn't consider those strikeouts failures—instead, he learned from them and prepared for the next at-bat. Don't be afraid of striking out.

WORDS FROM THE WISE

"He who never made a mistake never made a discovery."
—*Herman Melville*

Trust your intuition. We all have the remarkable gift of intuition—the ability to know or understand something without learning it or reasoning it through. The problem is, we often suppress our hunches and reject gut feelings because we're afraid of being wrong or being laughed at. Learn to trust your intuition. It won't always be right, but you'll be surprised at how often it is.

Be patient. Most problems—especially those in the workplace—can't be solved overnight. It takes time to find the facts, it takes time to brainstorm a solution, and it takes time to evaluate possible solutions to determine which is best. The larger the scope of the problem, the longer it will take to be solved. Keep this in mind when solving a mammoth problem, and take it one step at a time.

Practice:

Take another look at the typical responses to problems that opened up this chapter, then answer the questions that follow.

a. Run and hide.

b. Blame it on someone else.

c. Say it's not your problem; let someone else fix it.

d. Close your eyes and hope it goes away.

e. Shake your head and say, "Why me?"

1. What kind of problems cause you to react in any of these ways? Make a list of what you think are your problem-solving "problem areas" and describe your attitude toward facing those kinds of problems.

2. Now, make a list of problems you tend to solve successfully. What kind of problems are they? What is your attitude when you face these problems?

3. Compare your answers to questions 1 and 2. Note especially how your attitude is different when facing the first and second groups of problems.

ATMOSPHERE

You have the right attitude. You're all set to sit down and solve your problem. But it's midnight and you're exhausted, you didn't have any dinner, you have a headache, and you're still in a suit and uncomfortable new shoes. As wonderful as your attitude toward problem solving may be, you're not headed on the road to success if you try to solve your problem in this condition. Our mental and physical states both need to be optimized to enhance our chances for problem-solving success. So before you tackle a problem, consider your *environment* and your *mental and physical state*.

Environment. Conduct as much of your problem solving as possible in a setting that enhances your energy level and creativity. In what kind of atmosphere are you most productive? Consider:

- **Lighting.** Do you need bright light to keep you focused and aware? Or does the glare of a fluorescent bulb irritate you?

- **Furnishings.** Do you need a comfortable couch or chair, or do you tend to nod off if you're too comfortable?

- **Background noise.** Do you need the din of a noisy place to drown out other thoughts, or do you need peace and quiet? Do you think best with music (what kind?), or do you prefer silence?

Know the environmental conditions under which you work best and make an effort to meet those conditions when you must solve a problem.

Your mental and physical state. Your mental and physical states are intimately connected and are constantly affecting one another. If you sit down to confront a problem on an empty, growling stomach, for example, chances are you won't be thinking as effectively as you could be. So make sure your stomach is satisfied (but don't down a five-course meal right before a problem-solving session, or most of your energy will go to digesting, not to thinking). Similarly, if you're tired, stressed, or feeling overwhelmed, take a breather to regain mental balance. Go for a brisk walk. Shut your office door and stretch, slowly and deliberately, releasing the tension and letting the energy flow to your muscles. Clear your head by focusing on your body for a few minutes. You'll feel remarkably rejuvenated and ready for your problem-solving challenge. If there's a time of day when you are most energetic and creative, take advantage of it and schedule your problem solving for that time.

Practice:

1. Describe the kind of environment in which you are most productive.

2. Get to know your optimal mental and physical state. Answer the following:

    a. How much sleep do you need?

    b. What time of the day do you work best?

    c. What can you do in 10 minutes or less to release stress?

In Short

Effective problem solvers approach problems with a positive attitude. They face reality, embrace challenges, trust their intuition, and practice patience. They also optimize their mental and physical state by conducting the problem-solving process in an environment that enhances their productivity and creativity.

Skill Building Until Next Time

1. If you have control over your work space, make whatever changes you can to create an environment that will enhance your productivity and creativity.
2. Pay particular attention to your intuition over the next week. What does your "gut" tell you? Listen to your instincts and follow up on your hunches. (Be careful not to second-guess yourself.) How often were your hunches right?

CHAPTER | 7

REKINDLING YOUR CURIOSITY

Curiosity may have killed the cat but it certainly has saved many businesses and led to discoveries and inventions that have saved many lives. This chapter will explain the importance of observation in problem solving and give you strategies for rekindling your curiosity.

WORDS FROM THE WISE

"Curiosity is one of the most permanent and certain characteristics of a vigorous intellect."
—*Samuel Johnson*

Spend an afternoon with a four-year-old and you'll soon lose count of how many times the child asks, "Why?" Unfortunately, by the time children turn into adolescents, this wonderful sense of curiosity is often stifled—they become afraid to ask questions. This is a great shame, for people with a strong sense of curiosity are actively engaged with the world around them. They notice things, question things, learn things, and create things on a daily basis. And in the process, they develop outstanding problem-solving skills.

To improve your problem-solving skills, then, do as four-year-olds do: look with genuine wonder and curiosity at the world around you.

STOP, LOOK, AND LISTEN

Curiosity begins with the simple but often under-used act of observation. After all, you can't be curious about something you don't notice. Unfortunately, many of us go through much of our lives with our eyes half closed. That is, we see just enough to get us through the day, but we don't notice the details in what's around us. For example, take a look at the following questions. How many can you answer without checking?

- What was your spouse or roommate wearing before you left for work this morning?
- What color eyes do your parents have?
- Do your colleagues wear glasses?
- What do the ceilings in your office look like?
- Can you describe the landscape in front of your office building?
- Where are the smoke detectors or fire alarms in your office?

These questions may seem unimportant, but they serve an important purpose: They point out how little most people notice about the world around them.

Why Is Observation Important?

When we pay attention to the world around us, several important things happen. First, we see things that others may overlook. Second, when we notice things, especially unusual things, we naturally begin to wonder about them. Third, when we begin to question things—especially things that others have not even noticed—we can find problems (or situations that have the potential to become problems) and address them.

Take Sam, an assistant to the office manager, as an example. He noticed that one of the vendors included, in very small print at the bottom of the order form, a delivery surcharge of $20 for any item over 15 pounds. By noticing the charge and switching to another vendor, Sam saved the company hundreds of dollars in delivery surcharges.

In short, observation enables us to:

1. See what others don't see.

2. Ask useful questions.

3. Find problems and potential problems.

Practice:

Part I: If you are at home, describe your office or work area in as much detail as possible. If you are at work, describe your bedroom in as much detail as possible. Include sizes, shapes, colors, and, of course, objects.

Part II: After you've completed your description, take it to your office or your home and compare the description to the reality. How much did you notice? How accurate was your description? How much did you miss?

Asking Questions

If curiosity springs from observation, it blossoms with the act of asking questions. Say, for example, you notice that the equipment on the production floor is laid out in a square rather than in rows. Ask why. What led to that decision? What are the benefits of this layout ? What are the drawbacks? Maybe your observation and your questions will lead to a new, improved equipment layout.

By asking questions, as we mentioned above, you can spot problems and potential problems. And there's another benefit: Your constant questioning will lead you to answers, and you will be more knowledgeable about your workplace and your world.

Practice:

Choose an object—something on your desk or in your workspace—and list as many questions as possible about that object. For example:

Object: stapler

Questions:

- Who invented the stapler? When?

- What inspired that person to invent the stapler?

- What did people use to fasten papers together before someone invented the stapler?

- What do people who don't use staplers today use to fasten papers?

- What are the staples themselves made of? Could they be made of plastic or a material that's biodegradable?

- How could stapler design be improved to help prevent staples from jamming?

- Could a stapler be designed to use different-sized staples at the switch of a button?

- Do any staplers include a stapler remover feature? If not, could they?

Object:

Questions:

Practice:

The surgeon-turned-writer Lewis Thomas, in a wonderful essay entitled "Seven Wonders" (in *Late Night Thoughts on Listening to Mahler's Ninth Symphony*, 1980), lists the seven things he wonders about the most. A scientist fascinated by the human body and the natural world, Thomas includes *oncideres* (a species of beetle) and the scrapie virus (an infectious disease of adult sheep) on his list. What are your seven wonders? List them, along with some of your questions about those wonders, below.

Example:

1. I wonder about *sleep*. What happens in our brains when we fall asleep? Why do we need sleep? Why do some people need eight hours a night and others only four or five? Do all animals sleep? Why do the elderly need less sleep than the young? Why do we dream only in our sleep? What causes us to dream? Why do we have different cycles of sleep? Why do some people sleepwalk?

My Seven Wonders:

1.

2.

3.

4.

5.

6.

7.

WORDS FROM THE WISE

"Life was meant to be lived, and curiosity must be kept alive. One must never, for whatever reason, turn his back on life."
—*Eleanor Roosevelt*

In Short

An active sense of curiosity is vital to effective problem solving. Build your curiosity by being observant. Ask questions—who, what, when, where, why, and how. A habit of looking carefully at the world around you will enable you to see things that others don't see—and to find and address situations before they become problems.

Skill Building Until Next Time

1. Do some research. Find the answers to some of the questions on your Seven Wonders list.
2. Be especially observant for the next few days. Keep your eyes (and ears) open; look at everything around you. Share some of your observations with others. Chances are, they've never noticed much of what you'll see.

CHAPTER | 8

A MATTER OF PERSPECTIVE

How we see a problem determines the kind of solution we'll develop for that problem. That's why it is critical to
consider a problem from various points of view. This chapter
explains point of view and provides exercises to help you broaden your
perspective.

Six blind men come upon an elephant. Using their sense of touch, they
feel the animal to determine what it is. One man feels the animal's side
and says, "It must be a wall." Another feels the elephant's trunk and says,
"It must be a snake." Another feels the elephant's tail and decides, "It's a
rope." A fourth feels the elephant's ear and says, "It's a giant fan." A fifth
man feels the elephant's leg and announces, "It's a tree." Finally, the sixth
blind man feels the elephant's tusk and calls the creature a spear.

A wall, a snake, a rope, a fan, a tree, a spear—how could each of these
six men come up with such vastly different interpretations of the

elephant? The answer is clear: What we see and how we feel depends entirely upon our *perspective*.

Perspective is the point of view or position from which a person sees, experiences, or understands another person, place, or thing. In any given situation, there are always many different perspectives—and all are equally valid. Perspectives aren't right or wrong—they simply reflect the way we see the world. And because we all have different experiences and backgrounds, we all have a unique perspective.

Understanding that different perspectives exist is essential to effective problem solving. Imagine, for example, a conflict between two co-workers, Fran and Manuel. Fran is angry because she thinks Manuel was trying to get her in trouble by telling their boss something she had told Manuel in private. From Manuel's point of view, however, telling their boss was a way to help Fran. Was Manuel out-of-line? Various people will have various ways of seeing the situation depending upon their relationship with either Fran or Manuel and their position in the company. For example, Fran and Manuel's manager will see the conflict in a unique way because she is the one who must mediate the dispute. Background and experiences will affect how any third party sees the situation as well. For instance, someone who also had the experience of trying to help but being misunderstood might sympathize with Manuel.

When it comes to problem solving, it is important to be able to see a situation from many different perspectives. The six blind men, for example, were unable to solve the "problem" of the elephant—unable to see the elephant for what it was—because each of them had a specific, and very limited, point of view. We, too, are often guilty of this type of "tunnel vision," and as a result only see part of the picture (a trunk or tail or ear) instead of the whole thing (an elephant). For the manager to effectively solve the problem between Fran and Manuel, for example, she needs to be able to see the situation from *both* of their points of view while also considering her own perspective as a manager. Otherwise, her solution will probably be lopsided, and, as a result, not a very effective solution.

WORDS FROM THE WISE

"Some men see things as they are and ask, 'Why?' I dream things that never were and ask, 'Why not?'"
—*Robert F. Kennedy*

BROADENING YOUR PERSPECTIVE

With a little practice, you can learn to look at all kinds of things (not just problems) from various points of view. Let's begin with the following exercise:

Practice:

1. Look carefully at the drawing below. What do you see?

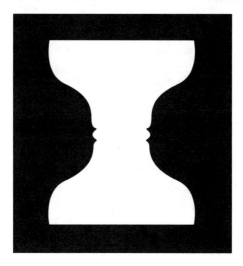

Answer:

What you see depends upon how you look at the drawing (your perspective). You might have seen one or both of the following:

1. Two faces nose-to-nose

2. An hourglass or goblet

In this type of exercise, it's often easy to see one of the images, but not so easy to see the other, until it's pointed out to us. Once we're able to see both images, however—once we've broadened our perspective—it's easy to see how both images are part of the drawing, and we can jump back and forth between the two perspectives. Our ability to "see," as a result, has expanded.

Practice:

Scenario: A train is pulling into the station. How do you "see" this event in each of the following cases?

1. You are a grandparent. On the train is your grandchild, whom you are going to see for the first time.

2. You are a parent about to send your only child off to college on the train.

3. You are that child about to go off to college and live away from home for the first time.

Answer:

Though all of these people are looking at the same thing (the incoming train), how each person *sees* the train—what it means to them, how they feel about it—is far from being the same. The grandparent, for example, will look at the train with great anticipation and excitement. The parent, on the other hand, will probably look at the train with mixed emotions—sadness, fear, hope, pride, perhaps some relief as well. The college-bound child, meanwhile, will probably look at the train with excitement, fear, anticipation, and relief—but for different reasons. Thus, as you can see, situations aren't set in stone; their interpretations can vary dramatically depending on what perspective they're viewed from.

PERSPECTIVE AND PROBLEM SOLVING

The ability to see situations from various points of view is essential for effective problem solving. You need to consider the problem from the perspectives of all those involved in order to best determine the cause of the problem and find the most effective solution. Imagine, for example, that you have the following problem:

> **Current situation:** You recently got a promotion, and your co-workers don't talk to you anymore.

> **Desired situation:** How can you get your co-workers to treat you like they did before your promotion?

If you look at this situation only from your own point of view, chances are you're not going to come up with an effective solution. Why? Because you're only considering *your* feelings and *your* relationship to the situation. This makes it easy to jump to conclusions about your co-workers. You might assume, for example, that they don't talk to you anymore because they're jealous; after all, you now earn more money, have more responsibility, and wield more authority.

But stop and think about the situation from *their* point of view. Perhaps it seems to them that *you've* been treating *them* differently since you got the promotion. Or perhaps they do treat you differently, but for good reason. Maybe they are afraid that others will think they're looking for special treatment if they continue to associate with you now that you're in a position of authority. Or they're afraid that you'll think they're not working hard enough if they take time out to chat.

In any case, unless you consider the problem from their point of view, and attempt to see the situation as *they* may see it, you're not likely to come up with an effective solution. You can't fix the problem if you don't understand *why* they've been treating you differently. And you can't figure out why they've been treating you differently until you put yourself in their shoes.

Putting Yourself in Someone Else's Shoes

Looking at a situation from other points of view not only expands your understanding of the problem, it also increases your ability to empathize with others. When you understand that problems affect different people in different ways, and you *actively imagine* the situation from those different points of view, you develop a much clearer understanding of the scope of the problem and are much more likely to come up with a solution that is not only effective, but considerate and fair.

Practice:

Consider the following problem from the point of view of each person involved.

> **Current situation:** Many employees are not getting phone messages, and the ones they're getting often have incorrect names or numbers.

> **Desired situation:** How can we make sure all employees get all of their phone messages in a timely and accurate manner?

> **Key facts:** There is only one receptionist and 10 incoming lines, most of which are busy at any given moment. There is no automatic voice-mail system.

1. The receptionist:

2. A potential client:

3. An employee:

Answers:

Answers will vary. The key to this exercise is to acknowledge that each of the three people will have very different ideas about the problem. For example:

1. **The receptionist:** The phones are constantly busy and I'm only one person! Of course I'm going to miss calls and get information wrong when I have people on hold and five lines running! I'm not super-woman. I need help!

2. **A potential client:** I keep leaving messages that no one returns. I guess this company doesn't want my business.

3. **An employee:** I know the receptionist is really busy but I can't believe how many messages I get with names and numbers mixed up. If this

continues, I'm going to lose clients. I'd like to have some control over calls that come in for me.

In Short

To develop the most effective solution to a problem, you need to be able to see the "big picture." That means seeing the problem from various points of view before you begin to brainstorm for a solution. Considering the problem from the point of view of each person involved will give you a better understanding of the problem and will enable you to develop a solution that is effective and fair.

Skill Building Until Next Time

1. Listen to others describe their problems. Do they stop to consider various points of view?
2. Think back to problems you have faced where you neglected to consider other perspectives. What happened as a result? What situations have you been in where others neglected to consider your point of view? What happened as a result?

CHAPTER | 9

IGNITING YOUR CREATIVITY, PART I

Effective problem solvers know that creativity plays an essential role in the problem-solving process. This chapter explains what creativity is, why it's important to the problem-solving process, and how you can release your creative energies.

Look carefully at the figure below. What is it?

Answer: _____

Chances are you said it's a triangle. And it is. But it could also be a slice of pizza, a piece of pie, a wedge, an arrowhead, a pencil point, a pyramid, a nose, a dunce cap, a mountain, an upside-down ice cream cone, the tip of an iceberg, a cat's ear, a tent, a teepee, a fang. . . .

The more creative you are, the more answers you can come up with for this question. It's all a matter of opening your mind, looking beyond the obvious, and seeing new possibilities.

WHAT IS CREATIVITY?

Creativity is the ability to imagine or develop original ideas or things. We might all be able to solve a simple problem, but a creative person will be able to develop a solution that is unique (and uniquely effective) because he or she has the ability to "see" things differently.

Instead of simply taking the standard approach to problems, instead of accepting the standard notions of boundaries and limits, creative people reach out beyond the "normal" modes of thinking to see the problem or situation in a new way. They see connections and relationships that others often don't; they ask questions that others might not think to ask; they are able to see things from a variety of perspectives; they are endlessly curious; and they trust in their ability to come up with ideas and solutions.

The Creativity Muscle

If you don't exactly fit the description above, don't despair—it doesn't mean you're not a creative person. While some people are inherently more creative than others, we *all* have the capacity to be extremely creative. Unfortunately, many of us bury our creative energies under layers of fear. We're often afraid to share our ideas because we're afraid that we'll be ridiculed or misunderstood.

Creativity is like a muscle. If it's not exercised regularly, it will atrophy. So if you've been afraid to use your creative skills, you probably have a lot of work to do—chances are your "muscle" is not in particularly good shape. If, on the other hand, you use your creativity muscle on a regular basis, it will be strong and limber, ready for action. That's why an active sense of curiosity and an ability to see things from various points of view are so important to creativity. They do for creativity what daily stretching does for the body—they keep you limber, ready to run with a new idea, make new connections, see things in an exciting and innovative way.

WORDS FROM THE WISE

"Creativity is inventing, experimenting, growing, taking risks, breaking rules, making mistakes, and having fun."
—*Mary Lou Cook*

Why Creativity is Important to Problem Solving

Guess what characteristic distinguishes those who are naturals at problem solving from those who struggle to find solutions? *Creativity*. Why? Because creativity is the key to determining *how* to get from the current situation to the desired situation. In any given situation, there are endless possibilities. The more creative you are, the more possibilities you can uncover. And the more possibilities you uncover, the more likely you are to find the best solution for that situation. If you can only think of one way to solve the problem, then you only have one choice. However, if you can think of twenty ways to solve the problem, then you have twenty options, and you can choose the one that solves the problem most effectively.

But creativity enables you to do much more. Creative problem solving will lead you to develop solutions that not only solve the problem (get you to the desired situation), but solve the problem in a way that solves *other* problems, prevents problems from recurring, and/or improves other situations. A creative problem solver, then, is someone who finds a solution that is original, imaginative, innovative—and, of course, effective.

For example, take a look at how Janet solved her problem. She was constantly losing her files on her desk and unable to find the information she wanted. To solve this problem, she could have simply created alphabetical files for all of her information. True, that would have fixed the situation. But Janet found a more creative, and, for her, more effective solution. She decided to divide her workspace into areas that connected the physical location of the files with their status. Thus:

- Things that were *high* priority—current projects—were kept in a *high* space: above her head.

- Things that had to be done *right* away were kept above her head and to the *right*.

- Things that could be *left* alone for the time being (but were still active) she kept above her head to the *left*.

- Things that were *low* priority—inactive files—were kept in a *low* place and filed below her desk on the *left*, because they were files with nothing *left* to be done.

- Finally, below her desk to the *right* were her "*right* hand" files—company policies and procedures, various human resources and payroll forms, etc.

How to Build Your Creativity Muscle

You can begin building your creativity muscle right away simply by opening your eyes and looking carefully at the world around you. Be observant! The more observant you are—the more you see of the world around you—the more open you will be to seeing things differently and making connections between things that at first may not seem related. And the more observant you are, the more you will naturally stimulate your sense of curiosity.

But an active sense of curiosity won't help build your creativity if you're afraid to ask questions. That's why it's essential to *stop being afraid*. Easier said than done, of course. But begin by remembering that when it comes to creativity, there's no such thing as a "right" or "wrong" answer or "good" or "bad" ideas. The only measure of quality is whether or not the idea can be applied to the current situation. And remember—if an idea doesn't work in the current situation, it may be the key to the solution of your next problem.

So let yourself go! In the exercises in this and the next chapter, tap into your creativity. Flex those muscles. Be open. Think freely. Don't censor yourself. And have fun! Let yourself be energized by the creative process.

Practice: Stretching Limits

List as many uses as possible for the objects below. Think beyond the norm. Use your imagination! Think of unusual situations in which the object might be used in different ways. We've provided an example for each to get you started.

Object: Paper clip

Uses: *hair pin*

Object: Empty soda bottle

Uses: *vase*

Practice: Making Connections

Write a sentence for each of the pairs of words below. Don't worry—they don't have to make sense! In fact, the more unusual, the better.

Example:

Words: *banana, tow truck*

Sentences: The tow truck was the color of a ripe banana.

                The driver of the tow truck ate a dozen bananas.

                The tow truck ate a banana.

                The banana chased the tow truck down the road.

1. *umbrella, chewing gum*

2. *whisker, trapeze*

3. *calendar, screw driver*

4. *video, green bean*

5. *brief case, dragon*

Practice: Visualization

Imagine that you are the following objects. What is your life like? How do you feel? What do you see?

Example:

Object: *an ant*

- I am strong—the strongest creature on earth. Go, go, go, go—I have work to do. No time to think or play. Forage, return. Forage, return. Forage, return. I know my duties. I fulfill them. I never question. I am a provider. I have a very keen sense of smell—if food is anywhere nearby, I can find it. My skin is hard and protective; rain drops may pound me but I don't even get wet.

1. *a ray of sunlight*

2. *a spoon*

In Short

We all have the capacity to be creative—to come up with original, imaginative ideas. Creativity is essential to the problem-solving process. The more creative you are, the more potential solutions you'll develop, and the more effective and innovative your solution will be. Stretch your creative muscles by being observant and asking questions.

Skill Building Until Next Time

1. Take a long walk with no other purpose than to just *look* carefully at the world around you.
2. Restart a creative hobby you used to have but have been "too busy" to enjoy. Or try something creative that you've always wanted to do: take an art class, dance lessons, a photography workshop.

CHAPTER | 10

IGNITING YOUR CREATIVITY, PART II

Stress, distractions, or just a plain lack of inspiration can give even the best of us "problem-solver's block." This chapter offers suggestions for how to break that block and find your creative energy.

WORDS FROM THE WISE

"Imagination is more important than knowledge."
—*Albert Einstein*

It is our imagination—our creativity—that enables us to make effective use of our knowledge and solve problems effectively. Even if you consider yourself a creative person, though, there are bound to be times when it's difficult to get your creativity flowing. When that happens, try one of the following strategies to re-start your creative energies:

Go for a walk. Get some fresh air. Out in the open, with your blood flowing, away from your office, you will be able to clear your head so you can think more effectively. And the fact that you are outside, breathing fresh air, will stimulate your creativity. You're bound to be inspired, either by nature and the forms of life around you, or by the creative work of others displayed in the architecture and sculptures of your town or city.

Change the scenery. If you can't take a break and get outside, change the scenery. Move out of your office and into an empty conference room. If you can concentrate with background noise, try the lunchroom or lounge. Whatever your options may be, a change of scenery is often enough to create a shift in your mentality. A new environment will open up new thoughts.

Look to others for inspiration. Do you have a favorite artist, musician, poet? Let them inspire you. Hang a poster of your favorite painting on the wall in your office. Tack your favorite poem on your bulletin board or tape it to your computer screen. Play your favorite opera or symphony as you sit down to solve a problem. Use the creative power of others to get your own creative juices flowing.

Try a creativity exercise like the ones you did in the last chapter and the ones you'll do next. These quick exercises can be the jump start you need to ignite your creativity.

MORE CREATIVITY EXERCISES

If you doubt your ability to think creatively, consider for a moment your dreams. When you sleep, your subconscious—which is free from the inhibitions that govern you during the day—comes alive in the form of dreams. Your dreams are evidence of your imaginative powers. You can tap into this power during your waking hours, too. Here's one exercise to show you how.

Practice: The Power of Dreams

In the space below, write down a dream—not a dream that you've actually had, but a dream that you make up here and now *as you write it*. Start with the words "Last night I dreamt" and create this dream from your imagination. Remember, it's a dream, so there are no rules—*anything* can happen!

As we've said, creative people have the ability to see things differently—to look at things with new eyes, as if they've never seen them before, as if they don't know the "rules" that determine the status quo. Here's an exercise to help you "break the mold" and see things differently.

Practice: Thinking Differently

For each of the words or phrases below, write a definition that is different from the word's actual meaning.

Example:

> *Light bulb:* A baby light beam. Plant bulb early in the spring to get a beautiful golden ray of light by mid-summer.

1. *bedrock:*

2. *bookcase:*

3. *earring:*

4. *brainstorm:*

MAKING CONNECTIONS

Another aspect of creativity is the ability to make connections, to see relationships between ideas and objects that most people don't see. One way writers express these kinds of connections is through the use of similes. Similes are comparisons of two distinct objects, like an office and a library or a briefcase and a Halloween candy bag:

Her office was as organized as a library shelf.
Her briefcase bulged like a child's Halloween candy bag.

There are many similes that have made their way into our vocabulary and become clichés (overused phrases). In the next exercise, you'll be challenged to revise those clichés so that they make new connections and create fresh images.

Practice: Making Connections

Revise the following clichés by creating a new comparison.

Example:

His hand was shaking <u>like a leaf</u>.
His hand was shaking *like a flagpole in a hurricane.*

1. She was quiet <u>as a mouse</u>.

2. The day went fast <u>as lightning</u>.

3. Her heart beat <u>like a drum</u> when she was introduced for her presentation.

In Short

When you find yourself struggling to think creatively, go for a walk or change the scenery to clear your head and get your ideas flowing. You can also look to other creative people for inspiration or try a creativity exercise to warm up to your task.

Skill Building Until Next Time

1. Choose an inspirational piece to place in your workspace—a poster of a work of art, a poem, a piece of music you can pop in the CD drive, a miniature reproduction of a sculpture—something you can have on hand to inspire you.
2. Keep a journal of your dreams for the next week or two. Write down everything you can remember. Let your subconscious be a source of your conscious creativity—and become aware of the power of your imagination.

FINDING A SOLUTION

In the first section of this book, you learned the first steps in the problem-solving process: identifying the problem (both the current and desired situations), determining its scope, prioritizing the parts of the problem, gathering facts, and summarizing the problem. In the second section, we discussed ways to develop a problem-solving disposition and stimulate your creativity. Now you're ready for the next step in the problem-solving process: determining a solution.

The chapters in this section will teach you various strategies for brainstorming solutions that will get you from the current situation to the situation you desire. You'll learn:

Σ Strategies for successful brainstorming sessions
Σ How to create a brainstorming list
Σ How to create a brainstorming map
Σ How to use random word association to make connections
Σ How to create a paradigm shift to think creatively about a problem

CHAPTER | 11

BRAINSTORMING SOLUTIONS, PART I

Now that you know how to define the problem, determine its scope, and research the facts, it's time to use your creativity and brainstorm for a solution. This chapter will define *brainstorming* and show you two effective brainstorming strategies.

Imagine a writer with a blank piece of paper and a pen. It is noon; he has been sitting at his desk, staring at the same blank page, since 8 a.m. By five, he is still there, slumped now in his chair, staring at a blank sheet of paper. Why? He can't think of what to write, so he writes nothing at all.

This illustration of "writer's block" should sound familiar; we've all experienced it in one form or another when we faced a creative task like writing, designing, or problem solving. We can't think of how to begin or what exactly to do or say, so we find ourselves paralyzed. In the end, we may end up completing the task, but it's not likely to be our best effort. It may feel forced, lack creativity, or lack effectiveness.

What can be done to break this kind of creativity block? The answer is simple: Just *begin*. Anywhere. With anything. In other words, *brainstorm*.

WHAT IS BRAINSTORMING?

Brainstorming is the act of free-flow idea production. When you brainstorm, your aim is to come up with as many ideas as possible in a short period of time. There's only one rule in brainstorming: anything goes. All ideas count, no matter how ridiculous they may seem. So don't censor, don't criticize, don't worry if something seems outlandish or absurd. It's an idea, and it may lead to another idea that may not be so ridiculous after all—it might, in fact, be the perfect solution.

You can brainstorm on your own or in groups. Brainstorming as a team can be a very powerful problem-solving tool. As the saying goes, two heads (or more) are better than one, and the more people you have brainstorming a solution, the more possible ideas you'll develop. Brainstorming in a group, however, has one drawback: Sometimes creativity is hindered because people are afraid of being ridiculed. Therefore it's critical for everyone in a brainstorming session to remember the "anything goes" rule. No idea should be categorized as stupid or useless. In a brainstorming session, *every* idea is a good one. This is important to remember even as you brainstorm on your own. Don't censor yourself. Every idea, no matter how strange, has the potential for genius.

The benefits of brainstorming are numerous. For one thing, just five minutes of brainstorming can save you five hours (or more!) of creativity block. Furthermore, brainstorming will give you a pool of ideas to chose from, and the more ideas you have to choose from, the greater the chance that the idea you choose will be highly effective. Your list of ideas also may come in handy for a future project.

There are many different brainstorming techniques. In the next three chapters, we'll cover four of them:

1. Listing

2. Mapping

3. Drawing connections

4. Out-of-the-box thinking

Listing

Do this right now: Without thinking, without stopping to come up with the "best" answer, list possible titles for a book or a movie that tells your life story. List as many titles as you can think of. Don't wait; start right now. Go.

Possible Titles:

How many names did you come up with? How long did it take you? Did you stop often, or did you keep going? How freely did your thoughts flow? Did you start right away, or hold off until you thought of a good starting point? Hopefully you were able to start right away and let your ideas flow freely. If not, however, don't worry—you just need to learn how to trust your ideas, and that will come with practice.

Now take a good look at your list. You'll probably notice several things. For instance, your first title may have been a pretty standard one, like the ones Ellen Raines, a legal secretary, came up with:

- The Life Story of Ellen Raines
- My Life Story
- The Biography of Ellen Raines

But as you brainstormed, something magical may have begun to happen. Because you did not inhibit yourself, because you let your mind work its magic, you began to get more creative. Maybe, by the end of your list, you were coming up with gems like these:

- When It Raines, It Pours
- Wonder Woman's Twin Sister, Separated at Birth
- Here Comes the Raines
- E.R.
- Pass the Hot Mustard, Please

Even though you might not like some of the ideas on your list, you should be able to see how one idea led to another and how the more ideas you put down, the more you were able to come up with. What are the chances you would have come up with some of the titles if you hadn't brainstormed? If out of a list of 20, 30, even 100, you have one truly fabulous idea, one that's just right for the situation, your brainstorming session was a success. It only takes one terrific idea to make brainstorming worthwhile. Meanwhile, other ideas on your list may come in handy at some other time.

WORDS FROM THE WISE

"I get the facts, I study them patiently, I apply imagination."
—*Bernard M. Baruch*

Practice:

Brainstorm a list of possible solutions to the phone message problem. We've reprinted the problem summary below. Remember, *no idea is a bad idea* when you're brainstorming.

> **Current situation:** Many employees are not getting phone messages, and the ones they're getting often have incorrect names or numbers.

Desired situation: How can we make sure all employees get their phone messages in a timely and accurate manner?

Key facts: There is only one receptionist and 10 incoming lines. There is no automatic voice-mail system.

Possible solutions:

Answers:

Answers will vary. Here's one possible list:

- Hire another receptionist.
- Disconnect the phone.
- Give everyone voice-mail.
- Get an answering machine that will go on when the receptionist is on another line.
- Hire a temp to help for the next few weeks until we come up with a more permanent solution.
- Reduce the incoming lines.
- Send the receptionist to a message-taking class.

- Install an electronic system so that when someone has a message, a light will go on at his or her computer.
- Have the receptionist type in messages via e-mail as she's speaking on the phone (eliminate paper messages).
- Have an automated answering system with a directory.
- Hire someone to run messages to employees every hour.
- Have every employee play receptionist for a day to find out what it's like.

As you can see, some of these ideas are far from practical. The last idea, for example, is interesting to be sure, and it might help employees empathize with the receptionist, but it won't lead to the desired situation. The list, however, includes a number of potential solutions. The next step (which we'll talk about in Section IV) is to evaluate the solutions and choose the one that will be most effective.

In Short

Brainstorming is the process of allowing a free flow of ideas—answers to a question, solutions to a problem. Brainstorming sessions will be most effective if you remember that anything goes; no idea is bad or stupid. Every idea counts. Listing (creating a list of ideas) is one of the most basic and effective techniques for brainstorming.

Skill Building Until Next Time

1. Use listing to brainstorm for different situations throughout the week, such as what to give someone as a gift, what to make for dinner, what to include in a report, and, of course, how to solve a problem.

CHAPTER | 12

BRAINSTORMING SOLUTIONS, PART II

There are many ways to stimulate the flow of ideas. This chapter demonstrates two more brainstorming strategies: mapping and drawing connections.

Listing is probably the most "open" or free-flowing brainstorming strategy. There are other techniques you can use that are more structured but still stimulate creative, free-flowing ideas. Let's look at two of those strategies: mapping and drawing connections.

MAPPING

Mapping is similar to listing, but with two key differences: mapping is much more visual and enables you to see relationships between different ideas more clearly. Mapping could be considered the "connect-the-dots" of brainstorming.

To being a mapping session, put the *desired situation* in a circle in the middle of the page (use a blank sheet of paper to give yourself plenty of room). Here's how we used mapping to brainstorm solutions for the following problem:

Current situation: You are a bank teller. One of the customers consistently chooses your window and asks you for a date every time, refusing to take "no" for an answer.

Desired situation: How can you get the customer to stop harassing you?

Key facts: The customer has been with the bank for 10 years and knows your manager well. The customer is also married (you are not).

Map

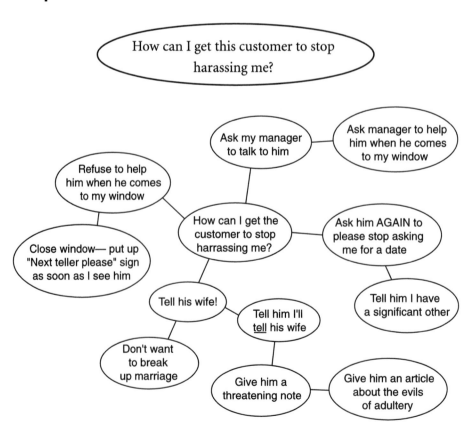

You'll notice that with a map, you might get into more detail than you would with a list. For example, notice how "telling his wife" leads to the thought "don't want to break up a marriage." You can also see how with a map, ideas are "grouped," whereas in a list, they're not. In this way, maps allow you to see how one idea relates to another. Now it's your turn.

WORDS FROM THE WISE

"Every child is an artist. The problem is how to remain an artist once he grows up."
—*Pablo Picasso*

Practice:

Draw a map of possible solutions to the following problem:

> **Current situation:** One of your co-workers is constantly gossiping about others in the office.

> **Desired situation:** How can I get him to stop sharing gossip with me?

> **Key facts:**
> - Your desks are right next to each other.
> - You have only been on the job one year; he's been there ten.

Your map:

How can I get him to stop sharing gossip with me?

DRAWING CONNECTIONS

The *drawing connections* brainstorming strategy involves drawing connections between random words and your problem. Begin by writing down three or four random words. The words must be random; avoid consciously choosing words that are directly related to the problem at hand. No matter how distant the words may seem, your mind will be able to find some sort of connection between those words and your problem.

Once you've chosen your words, your task is to relate each word to your problem. Again, this is a brainstorming exercise, so no connection that you see can be wrong. Anything goes. So for each word, begin writing freely, trying to draw connections to your problem. Here's an example:

> **Current situation:** I have two reports due tomorrow and haven't started either one.

> **Desired situation:** How can I get them done (and done well) on time?

> **Key facts:**
> - Both reports are minutes of meetings held earlier in the week.
> - Both meetings were about one hour.
> - I have extensive notes from the meetings.
> - I have meetings and projects scheduled for the entire day today.

> **Random words:**
> - island
> - toast
> - calendar

Brainstorm

> *Island:* No man is an island. . . Maybe I don't have to do this alone. Can I get someone to help? I do have detailed notes, and Renee has done meeting minutes for me before. Islands are surrounded by water. I feel

like I'm drowning. Too much work. What work can I delegate? Can I create a template for these minutes so that I just have to fill in the blanks each week?

Toast: I'm toast if I don't get these minutes done. I like toast with butter and jelly. Can I butter-up Jack to get extra time for my other projects?

Calendar: There aren't enough days in the year, there aren't enough hours in the day. Maybe I'll skip lunch and stay late—stretch my hours out. Take a careful look at my schedule—maybe I can get out of one of my meetings, or leave early. What if I came in early tomorrow?

Our minds have an amazing capacity for drawing connections and seeing relationships between things. Notice how this exercise generated a variety of possible solutions. Were you skeptical? Did you wonder how random words could be related to a problem so effectively? Now it's your turn:

Practice:

Use the drawing connections technique to brainstorm a solution for the following problem. (Notice how the desired situation is both specific and measurable.)

Current situation: I love my job but I don't earn enough money to pay all my bills and enjoy a little entertainment.

Desired situation: How can I earn a few hundred dollars more each month?

Key facts:
- Other companies pay more than yours for the work you do.
- You have very close friends at your current company and are very happy there.

- You are good at (list three things you are good at, such as *organizing*, *cooking*, and *planning*):

- _____
- _____
- _____

Random words: Choose three random words, then brainstorm connections to each.

1.

2.

3.

In Short

Mapping and drawing connections to random words are two effective brainstorming techniques. Use them to generate possible solutions for your problems and any other situation where you need to generate ideas.

Skill Building Until Next Time

1. Use the mapping and drawing connections techniques to brainstorm ideas for solutions to a particular problem this week. Notice how the two different techniques enable you to come up with very different ideas.

CHAPTER | 13

BRAINSTORMING SOLUTIONS, PART III

O ur beliefs about the world around us can sometimes limit our ability to think creatively. This chapter will
explain how we see the world through different *paradigms* and
how to create a paradigm shift to think about problems in a new way.

Sometimes we have trouble coming up with a creative solution because
we get stuck in one way of thinking about a problem. This occurs when
we're used to seeing that type of problem handled in a certain way. As a
result, we end up with a tunnel-vision perspective on the problem. We're
stuck inside the "box" of traditional experience because we see the problem through traditional *paradigms*.

PARADIGMS

Paradigms are ways of thinking about, perceiving, and understanding the
world around us. Whereas our *perspectives* are unique to each of us as

individuals, we often share paradigms because they are based upon a shared base of knowledge. For example, before Galileo Galilei proved that the sun was the center of the solar system, people throughout Europe believed that all of the planets *and* the sun revolved around the *earth*. But after Galileo proved that the earth was not in the center, the Western world underwent a serious paradigm shift as people realized the universe had a very different design (and people were less central to that design) than they'd imagined. After Galileo's discovery, people had to look at and understand the world—and their place in it—differently.

Here's a more recent example. For years, baby bottle manufacturers had been working to improve bottle design so that babies would swallow less air with their juice or milk. Improvement after improvement was made on the bottle nipples, and the changes were certainly beneficial, but air intake remained a problem because the bottle still had to be held at an angle. Finally someone broke out of the box—rejected the existing paradigm—and changed the *bottle* itself. Bottles now come with an angle *built in* to help reduce air intake.

Here are some other examples of major paradigm shifts that have affected our society:

OLD PARADIGM	NEW PARADIGM
Women belong at home.	Women are a vital part of the workforce.
Children should be seen and not heard.	It is important to acknowledge children's ideas and questions.
Organizations should be managed top-down.	Organizations are best managed bottom-up.

Notice that paradigms are much more than opinions, like "Jack Nicholson is a great actor." Paradigms are major beliefs we have that shape our perception of everyday people, places, and things. They are like frames through which we see the world.

Creating a Paradigm Shift

The trouble with paradigms is that they tend to be static and difficult to change. Often we hold on to paradigms that no longer match the reality of the changing world around us. This is unfortunate, since paradigms are often limiting. The frame through which we look at the world is often too small to permit freedom of thought. Creating a *paradigm shift* will help break open that frame, and free you from the paradigms that keep you thinking about a problem in a limited way.

To create a paradigm shift and think "out-of-the-box," you need to change one of the three key elements of the problem: the current situation, desired situation, or the key facts. If your change makes the problem absurd, so much the better—you'll be forced to think more creatively. As with any brainstorming session, some solutions won't be usable; some won't be realistic or even physically possible. But by stretching your mind and looking at the problem through a new frame of reference, you should be able to come up with very powerful ideas for solving your problem.

Here's an example to demonstrate this brainstorming strategy. Remember the phone message problem?

Current situation: Many employees are not getting phone messages, and the ones they're getting often have incorrect names or numbers.

Desired situation: How can we make sure all employees get all of their phone messages in a timely and accurate manner?

Key facts:

- There is only one receptionist and 10 incoming lines, most of which are busy at any given moment.
- There is no automatic voice-mail system.

To think out of the box, you might change the problem by adding the following fact:

Key facts:

- There is only one receptionist and 10 incoming lines, most of which are busy at any given moment.

- There is no automatic voice-mail system.

- *The receptionist speaks only Swedish.*

Now, with this odd key fact to consider, you can brainstorm and write freely about the problem. You might, for example, write something like the following:

- No wonder there's a problem! The receptionist and the employees aren't speaking the same language. And how can she understand the callers—or they understand her—if she only speaks Swedish? How much gets lost in the translation?

With this change in the problem, you're able to look at it in a different way: as a problem in *communication* rather than a problem with technology or human resources. Maybe the receptionist isn't clear about what the employees expect, or maybe the receptionist isn't familiar with the industry and doesn't understand the language of the business (the industry's jargon). As a result, he or she gets much of the information confused.

Now it's your turn to try. This time, we want you to include the *whole* problem-solving process we've discussed so far. We've listed a current situation below. Read it carefully, then:

1. Write a question expressing the desired situation.

2. Ask questions to determine the scope of the problem.

3. Cluster and prioritize those questions.

4. Research the facts. (Make up answers to your questions.)

5. Summarize the problem.

6. Make sure you have the right attitude and are in the right environment for brainstorming.

7. Create a paradigm shift to brainstorm for solutions.

Current situation: You are paid to work nine to five, with one hour for lunch and no overtime. Yet your boss often gives you work that you can't get done without staying late.

Desired situation:

Questions:

WORDS FROM THE WISE

"All good things which exist are the fruits of originality."
—*John Stuart Mill*

In Short

Paradigms are ways of looking at or understanding the world. You can create a paradigm shift to view a problem differently and more creatively. Simply change one part of the problem—something about the current situation, desired situation, or key facts—to force you to think about the problem in a new way.

Skill Building Until Next Time

1. Think about the paradigms that shape your understanding of the world. For example, do you believe that mothers should stay home with their children? That weekdays are for work and weekends for play?
2. Broadening your perspective will make it easier for you to create paradigm shifts. Think about ways that you can broaden your perspective.

SECTION | IV

EVALUATING YOUR SOLUTIONS

Now that you've brainstormed and have a series of possible solutions, it's time to determine which of those solutions will be the most effective. The chapters in this section will teach you the following techniques for evaluating potential solutions:

1. Simple ranking
2. Ranking by criteria
3. Pros and cons

You'll also learn how to avoid the following errors in reasoning during the evaluation process:

1. Appeals to emotion
2. Slippery slope
3. False dilemma
4. Circular reasoning
5. Non sequitur

CHAPTER | 14

EVALUATING SOLUTIONS, PART I

I t's not always easy to know which solution is the best one for the problem you're facing. That's why it's important to develop specific criteria for evaluating each of the possible solutions you formulate in your brainstorming session. The next two chapters will show you strategies for determining those criteria and effectively evaluating your solutions.

Imagine you have a boss who constantly puts you down in front of others. You want him to stop this behavior, but you don't want to risk losing your job. You brainstorm the following solutions to this problem:

1. Tell him to take this job and shove it.

2. Start ignoring him when he insults you.

3. Tell him, in private, that his insults make it difficult for you to have the right attitude to work for him productively.

4. Start insulting him back to show him how it feels.

5. Give him a letter asking him to stop putting you down.

Which is the best solution? Which should you choose to implement?

In this case, it's quite clear which solution would most likely get you the results you desire: solution 3. However, it isn't always this easy to spot the best solution. Often, your brainstorming session will provide you with several solutions that are feasible and potentially very effective. Solution 5, for example, might work well also. If more than one solution seems likely to do the trick, how do you decide which solution to implement?

SIMPLE RANKING

One of the easiest ways to determine the best solution is to do a simple ranking: Look carefully at the solutions and then rank them from 1 to 5, 1 being the best solution, 5 the worst. Even if it's clear from the start which solution is best, ranking the solutions can be helpful, since the solution that seems the best at the outset may not prove to be feasible, in which case you'd consider solution 2.

Practice:

Rank the solutions to the problem in the previous example. Be sure you can explain your ranking.

1 = Best Solution   5 = Worst Solution

_____ Tell him to take this job and shove it.

_____ Start ignoring him when he insults you.

_____ Tell him, in private, that his insults make it difficult for you to have the right attitude and work for him productively.

_____ Start insulting him back to show him how it feels.

_____ Give him a letter asking him to stop putting you down.

Answers:

The best solution is probably the third, to talk to him in private and explain how his behavior affects you. The second best would be to deal with the problem in writing. Face to face is better, but at least a letter still directly addresses the problem. However, if your boss is very intimidating and will make you too uncomfortable to explain yourself clearly in a face-to-face situation, then solution 5 is probably best.

How you rank the remaining three choices will vary; all are troublesome. The first is probably the least effective because it won't lead you to the desired situation, which is to keep your job. The fourth is not effective because it too is likely to get you fired. And the second solution may end up creating more tension. Although ignoring him might call attention to his troublesome behavior, he may get angry (or angrier)—and that could cost you your job.

HOW DO YOU KNOW WHAT'S "BEST"?

In the previous exercise, you ranked the solutions according to what you determined was the *best* solution. Generally speaking, "best" means most likely to get you the desired situation. Sometimes, however, "best" isn't so easy to define. Best in what way? Quickest? Cheapest? Easiest to accomplish?

When different solutions can be described as "best" for different reasons, then a simple ranking won't be very helpful in determining the most effective solution. You need instead to rank the solutions according to various criteria. Once you rank the solutions for each characteristic, you can determine the best solution by seeing:

1. Which solution receives the best ranking overall, or
2. Which solution ranks well for the criteria that are most important to you.

For example, you might choose time and cost as the criteria that determine the best solution. Thus, the solution that ranks best in both of those categories is the one you should implement. Or both criteria may be important, but cost is the *most* important. Thus the solution with a very low ranking for cost and a low ranking for time is the one you should implement.

WORDS FROM THE WISE

"In many lines of work, it isn't how much you do that counts, but how much you do well and how often you decide right."
—*William Feather*

Common Criteria for Evaluation

While the criteria you use to measure the quality of each solution will vary from problem to problem, here are several categories that apply to almost any problem:

- **Effectiveness**: How likely is it that this solution will get me to the desired situation?

- **Feasibility**: How realistic is this solution? How likely is it that this solution could be effectively implemented?

- **Time**: How long will it take to implement this solution? How long will it take to get the desired results?

- **Cost**: How much will it cost (in money or other resources) to implement this solution?

- **Human resources**: How many people will need to be involved to implement this solution?

- **Difficulty/ease of implementation**: Overall, how easy or how difficult will it be to implement this solution?

- **Risk**: How much is at risk in implementing this solution?

Using a Table to Compare Rankings

Once you determine your criteria for ranking solutions, construct a simple table to help you keep track of the rankings. For example, look at the following chart. We've ranked three solutions to the phone message problem in order of effectiveness for each of three criteria: caller satisfaction, time to see results, and cost. Thus, the solution that is likely to create the greatest caller satisfaction gets a 1 in that column; the second best in that category gets a 2; and the third, a 3. We followed the same procedure for the other criteria to come up with the following totals:

SOLUTION	CALLER SATISFACTION	TIME TO SEE RESULTS	COST	TOTAL
Hire another receptionist.	2	2	1	5
Give everyone voice-mail so receptionist can transfer callers instead of taking messages.	1	1	2	4
Install an automated answering system with a directory and have callers speak to receptionist only at their request.	3	3	3	9

If you add up the scores for each solution, you can see that the solution with the lowest score is the best solution to this problem.

Let's take another look at this situation, though, under slightly different circumstances. Let's say you're on an extremely tight budget. In the previous ranking, all the criteria carried the same weight. Now, however, one of your criteria is clearly more important than others. To determine the best solution, then, you need to construct your table a little differently. Before you actually rank the solutions, you need to rank the *criteria* according to level of importance. In this case, the criteria rank as follows:

1. *Cost.* No matter how good the solution may be in other categories, we can't implement it if it costs too much money.

2. *Caller satisfaction.* We want our callers to be happy with the new system, even if it takes a little longer to see the results.

3. *Time.* As long as we see results within a month or two, we'll be happy.

Here's a revised table based on the ranking of the criteria. The totals may still be the same, but now the solution with the lowest total is not necessarily the best. Solution 1 has a higher score, but it is the best solution in terms of cost. The only way to decide which solution to implement now is to determine how much more important cost is than caller satisfaction.

SOLUTION	COST	CALLER SATISFACTION	TIME TO IMPLEMENT	TOTAL
Hire another receptionist.	1	2	2	5
Give everyone voice-mail so receptionist can transfer callers instead of taking messages.	2	1	1	4
Install an automated answering system with a directory and have callers speak to receptionist only at their request.	3	3	3	9

Practice:

Use the table method to determine the best solution out of those you brain-stormed in Chapter 12 for the problem of how to earn extra money each month (see page 106). For this exercise, limit the number of solutions to four, and follow the directions below:

1. Rewrite your solutions in the chart below.

2. Choose four criteria you wish to consider. For example, you might use: time required to find job, ease of work, pleasure of work, and pay per hour.

3. Rank those criteria.

4. Write the criteria in the table in order of rank.

5. Give each solution the appropriate rank.

6. Decide which solution is best.

SOLUTION:	CRITERION 1:	CRITERION 2:	CRITERION 3:	CRITERION 4:	TOTAL

Best solution: _____

In Short

To determine the best solution, you need to decide what you mean by "best." Are you judging for general effectiveness, or are there specific criteria, such as cost, time, and feasibility, that you need to consider? Determine those criteria, and rank them. Then, use a table to see how each solution ranks in each of these categories.

Skill Building Until Next Time

1. Think back to a recent problem where you chose one solution over another. How did you make your decision? Did certain criteria influence your decision? What were those criteria?
2. Use the ranking technique to determine the best solution to a problem you are currently facing. What is most important to you in terms of the solution? What criteria will you use to judge and rank your solutions?

CHAPTER | 15

EVALUATING SOLUTIONS, PART II

Another effective technique for evaluating the effectiveness of possible solutions is to carefully consider the pros and cons of each solution. This chapter explains the pro/con approach.

WORDS FROM THE WISE

"When you approach a problem, strip yourself of preconceived opinions and prejudice, assemble and learn the facts of the situation, make the decision which seems to you to be the most honest, and then stick to it."

—*Chester Bowles*

Allegra had a decision to make: "Should I ask for a raise when I have my performance review?" To help make sure she made the right decision, she decided to list the pros (benefits) and cons (drawbacks) of each choice—asking for a raise and not asking. In the end, she realized that even though she'd be uncomfortable asking, and even though the answer might be "no," the potential benefits of asking for a raise far outweighed the benefits of not asking. And there were fewer drawbacks to asking.

The process Allegra used to make her decision is one that is also very effective in determining which solution to implement. Allegra looked at her two choices (to ask and not to ask) and then carefully considered the pros and cons of each choice. As a result, she was able to see which choice had the most benefits and the fewest drawbacks. That choice—asking for the raise—then became the right "solution."

To apply this technique to the problem-solving process, simply create a pro/con chart for each possible solution. The chart is simple and should look something like the following:

Solution:

PROS	CONS

Put the solution at the top of the chart. Then, in the "pros" column, list each benefit you can think of for that solution. Similarly, in the "cons" column, list each drawback of the solution. Be sure to consider the solution from all angles. Think about the various criteria discussed in Chapter 14— time, money, feasibility, etc.—and any other criteria that are important or specific to the problem.

MEASURING PROS AND CONS

Once you've completed your pro/con chart for each solution, how do you determine which solution is best?

Generally speaking, any solution that has more items in the "cons" column than in the "pros" column is probably not an effective solution and should be discarded. However, there are times when one pro can be so powerful that it outweighs a dozen cons. That's why it's important to quantify each item on a pro/con list. That is, to gain a truer measure of the merit of each solution, assign each pro and con on the list a numerical value to show how important it is in relation to the problem. For example, look how we've weighed the pros and cons for two solutions below. Each item is measured on a scale of 1–10, 1 meaning of little weight or value, and 10 meaning of great weight or value.

Current situation: Your boss constantly puts you down in front of others.

Desired situation: How can I get him to stop putting me down without losing my job or increasing the tension between us?

Solution: Tell him, in private, that his insults make it difficult for you to have the right attitude and work for him productively.

PROS		CONS	
I'll be addressing the problem in the most direct manner possible, and that should earn his respect.	10	I'm very uncomfortable with him and I know he'll try to intimidate me if we're alone.	10
I'll be able to gauge his reactions and explain further if he doesn't seem to understand.	9	I might have trouble expressing myself clearly or forget to say certain things.	10
He'll see that I'm not afraid to stand up for myself and that I'm professional in the way I handle the situation.	9	I might lose my temper.	5
If he ridicules me, this time it'll be in private.	6	He might lose his temper.	6
I won't embarrass him by pointing out his behavior in front of others.	7		
I can rehearse what I want to say.	9		
Total:	**50**	**Total:**	**31**

Solution: Give him a letter asking him to stop putting you down.

PROS		CONS	
I can take my time composing my letter and won't have to worry about forgetting to say something.	10	He might misunderstand something I wrote and I won't be able to respond right away to set things straight.	9
He can't interrupt me.	9	He'll see that I'm afraid to talk to him about this and that I'm really intimidated by him.	9
I like to write.	2	He might ridicule me by passing my letter around.	5
Others might write similar letters if asked.	5		
Total:	**26**	**Total:**	**23**

Even though there aren't many cons listed for solution 1, notice how much weight the first two cons carry. Simply looking at the number of pros and cons in a list won't necessarily reflect how they measure up against one another. Imagine putting the pros and cons on a scale. You could have one pro and ten cons, but if that one pro is a gold nugget and the ten cons are each pieces of copper, your single pro will weigh more than all those pieces of copper.

With this method, then, each item in the pro/con list is weighed according to its importance or value, and that enables us to come up with a "score" for the pros and cons for each solution.

Practice:

1. Use this pro/con method to evaluate three possible solutions that you brainstormed in Chapter 12 for how you could earn a few extra hundred dollars each month.

Solution:

PROS		CONS	
Total:		Total:	

Solution:

PROS		CONS	
Total:		Total:	

Solution:

PROS		CONS	
	Total:		Total:

2. Based on your evaluation, which is the best solution?

In Short

Weighing the pros and cons of possible solutions is another effective way to determine which solution you should implement. Carefully consider the benefits and drawbacks of each solution and then give each pro and con the appropriate weight on a scale of 1–10. Add up your columns to see how the pros measure up against the cons for each solution and how the solutions compare.

Skill Building Until Next Time

1. Get into the habit of thinking in terms of pros and cons. Make a pros/cons list for a decision you have to make today.
2. Use the pro/con evaluation method to determine the best solution for a problem you're currently facing.

CHAPTER | 16

COMMON ERRORS IN REASONING, PART I

E ven when we have carefully evaluated all of our solutions, we sometimes may choose the wrong solution to implement. This chapter will explain three types of errors in reasoning that sometimes mislead us in the problem-solving process.

Sometimes, even though we follow the problem-solving procedure faithfully, we still end up picking a solution that is not the most effective. How does this happen?

When you've done everything else right and still picked the wrong solution to implement, chances are you committed one of many common errors in reasoning. The next two chapters will explain several of those errors in reasoning (also called *logical fallacies*) and tell you how to avoid them. In this chapter, we'll deal with several *appeals to emotion*.

APPEALS TO EMOTION

Your colleague, Geoff, wants you to switch your schedule with his next week so he can attend a playoff game with his children. When he asks you to make the switch, he says, "I've come to you first because I know you're the most considerate person in this entire office."

Even though it's a tremendous inconvenience to you, you say yes. Why? In part because Geoff succeeded in appealing to your emotions. That is, he appealed to your sense of vanity by making you feel good about yourself. His flattery helped him get what he wanted, even though it wasn't a wise decision for you.

While appeals to just about any emotion can cause us to make an error in judgment, the most common errors occur when the appeals are made to these four emotions:

- Fear
- Vanity
- Desire to belong
- Pity

All too often, when we're at that critical point in the problem-solving process of evaluating our solutions, we accept or reject solutions based not on evidence or good common sense but on how we feel, what we fear, or what we desire.

Flattery

They say flattery will get you nowhere, but all too often it gets people what they want—even when they don't deserve it. It often leads people to make poor decisions, especially in the problem-solving process.

Imagine, for example, that you are evaluating several possible solutions to a scheduling problem. Solution A would benefit your colleague Andre the most, solution B would benefit Brenda the most, and solution C would benefit Carol the most. When you rank each solution for the criteria of effectiveness, feasibility, and ease of implementation, solution B ranks highest. However, before you choose which solution to implement, Carol pulls you aside and says, "I'm really impressed with the way you're handling this schedule mix-up. Nice work!" The solution you implement? Solution C.

Now, Carol may or may not have been flattering you to get a solution that benefited her the most, and you may or may not have realized that your decision was influenced by her comment. But the fact is, you let her flattery influence your decision about which solution to implement, and as a result you did *not* choose the solution that had the most merit.

Scare Tactics

Scare tactics refers to the false reasoning that occurs when you make a decision based on what you are afraid *may* happen rather than on what you know to be true. Take the scheduling problem scenario again as an example. Instead of telling you what a wonderful job you're doing, Carol pulls you aside and says:

"I know you've been working hard to fix this scheduling problem. I sure hope I don't have to work more than one evening shift a week. By the way, it would really be a shame if everyone found out that you used to date the boss, wouldn't it?"

If you now choose to implement solution C instead of solution B, you'll have given in to another appeal to emotion—this time, your sense of fear. Worried that Carol will spread gossip if you don't implement the solution that is best for her, you choose to implement a solution that is less effective instead of the solution that has the most merit.

Keep in mind that scare tactics are very different from *warnings*. A warning acknowledges a real threat to your physical or emotional well being, in which case heeding it would be logical and reasonable. Scare tactics, on the other hand, lead you to make a decision that is *not* based in logic or reason— just fear. If the gossip Carol threatens to reveal could endanger your job, and it's *likely* that she'll carry out that threat, then it would *not* be a logical fallacy to implement solution C instead of solution B. The difference is that you *know* you're choosing the less effective solution for a personal and emotional reason, but you're doing so to protect your job. (On the other hand, there's always the possibility that your effectiveness on the job will be questioned if it's clear that you could have implemented a more effective solution.)

Peer Pressure

Along with fear and vanity, another extremely powerful emotion is our desire to be accepted by others. As children, we may have done things that we knew were wrong because of pressure from our friends. Unfortunately, many people continue to give in to peer pressure throughout their lives. This can be especially problematic when it comes to problem-solving: We make the mistake of thinking a solution is "best" because it is the one that someone else wants us to employ.

Let's return again to the scheduling problem. Imagine solution A redistributes the hours so that everyone works one night shift each week. Solution B gives each employee the day shift for three weeks and the night shift for one week each month. Solution C gives certain employees the day shift and other employees the night shift.

From your point of view, solution C has the most merit; it's the easiest to implement, will result in the least confusion, and provides the most stability in the schedule. A group of employees, however, has made it clear that they prefer solution B. Of course, it's in your best interest to keep your employees happy, but if you choose to implement solution B when solution C is much better just because it's what the employees want you to do, then you're giving in to peer pressure.

Similarly, if your two best friends are pressuring you to implement solution A (say, because it'll free you up for Tuesday night bowling), and you do, you've made your decision not based on logic but on your desire to do what will make your friends happy (and what will make them like you). A true friend, however, will appreciate that you've made the *right* decision by sticking with solution B.

Pity

There are many times when we are wise to make decisions based on our sense of pity and compassion for others. Sometimes, helping others is simply the right thing to do. But there are times when we make decisions that are *not* wise simply because we feel sorry for people involved. For example, you have several possible solutions to the scheduling problem and have determined that solution A, which distributes all hours evenly, is the solution that has the most merit. However, you know that Carol is a single mother with three children and no child support. If you choose to implement a solution that gives extra benefits to Carol—the most flexible hours, for example, or the most opportunity for overtime—you've made your decision based on your emotions (your sense of compassion for Carol) rather than on your sense of logic.

When it comes to pity, however, it's important to know that sometimes choosing a solution that makes sense emotionally is not always illogical or wrong. For example, if Carol has been a long-time employee and is very valuable to the company, and if a schedule that favors her doesn't put anyone else at a great disadvantage, then including your compassion for Carol in your evaluation process is probably the right thing to do.

WORDS FROM THE WISE

"He only employs his passion who can make no use of his reason."
—*Cicero*

Practice:
Do any of the following situations appeal to emotion rather than reason? If so, which emotion?

1. Solution A is the easiest to implement, but choosing solution B will give everyone on the team what they want.

2. Solution C is the least expensive and most likely to get the desired results, but solution A will keep Charlie from telling the boss about those sick days I took to go golfing.

3. Solution C isn't as effective as A or B, but it'll keep Mary from getting fired.

4. Louisa and Skip think solution B is the most effective, so it's probably the best to implement.

Answers:

1. Unless solution B is ineffective in every way other than giving everyone what they want, it's probably not an appeal to emotion. Whatever the problem, a solution that satisfies all parties is usually a good one, even if it's not as easy to implement as other solutions.

2. This is an appeal to fear (scare tactics).

3. This is an appeal to pity.

4. Letting Louisa and Skip's opinion dictate your decision is an example of peer pressure.

In Short

While our emotions are important and not to be ignored, they shouldn't determine which solution to implement. When fear, vanity, pity, or our desire to belong lead us to choose one solution over another, more effective solution, we've committed an error in reasoning.

Skill Building Until Next Time

1. Think carefully about the last decision you made. How much did your emotions influence your decision?

CHAPTER | 17

COMMON ERRORS IN REASONING, PART II

This chapter explains four more common errors in reasoning: slippery slope, false dilemma, circular reasoning, and non sequitur.

Logical fallacies come in many forms. Some appeal to your emotions, like the ones we discussed in the previous chapter. Others, however, are often harder to detect because they *appear* to be logical. Four such fallacies are *slippery slope, false dilemma, circular reasoning,* and *non sequitur.*

SLIPPERY SLOPE

You've been having a problem with employees stealing from the supply room.

"Although it makes the most sense to require supervisor approval to access the supply room," says your colleague Ed, "we can't implement that solution. If we do, next thing you know, we'll be required to get supervisor approval for everything, even just to go to the bathroom."

Has Ed saved you from future disaster, or led you down a path of error?

While what Ed said may seem to make sense, he's guilty of a very common error in reasoning: the *slippery slope.*

The slippery slope fallacy presents an if/then scenario. It argues that *if* X happens, *then* Y will follow. Sounds logical, right? But this "next thing you know" argument has one major flaw: X doesn't *necessarily* lead to Y. In order for you not to be guilty of slippery slope, X has to be *very likely* to lead to Y. Thus, before you make a decision based on an if/then scenario, you need to very carefully consider whether there's a logical relationship between X and Y.

Take a careful look at Ed's argument, for example. He claims that if you require employees to get supervisor approval for access to the supply room, then before you know it, supervisor approval will be required for everything. True, this *is* possible—the precedent of the supplies may lead to similar policies for all kinds of office functions. But how *likely* is it that this will happen? Not very, which means it's a slippery slope argument.

Here's another example. Your colleague, Renee, is constantly gossiping about other employees. One solution is to tell her that her gossiping makes you uncomfortable. And this is probably the most effective solution. However, it's easy to use slippery slope to talk yourself out of this solution and into another, less effective one. Here's how:

> If I tell Renee that her gossiping bothers me, then she'll probably stop talking to me altogether. I don't want that kind of silence or tension between us. I'll just avoid her as much as possible instead.

What's most likely going on here is that you are uncomfortable with confronting Renee, so you use slippery slope "reasoning" to talk yourself into another, less challenging and less effective solution.

FALSE DILEMMA

"Either you're with us, or you're against us. Which is it?"

Have you ever been put on the spot like this before, where you were forced to decide between two contradictory options? Chances are you have. But chances are you also had more choices than you thought.

The *false dilemma* fallacy aims to convince that there are only two choices: There is X and there is Y, and there is nothing in between. The "logic" behind this fallacy is that if you think there are only two choices, then you won't stop to consider other possibilities. Here's an example:

You have presented your colleague, Sam, with a list of four possible solutions to a problem. Sam takes one look at your list and says, "Well, forget ideas 1 and 4. It's either 2 or 3. Either we do it like we planned, or we don't do it at all."

Sam is making a big mistake. By discarding ideas 1 and 4, he failed to see that they actually improved upon the original plan by suggesting ways to save time and money.

CIRCULAR REASONING

You're evaluating possible solutions to a problem with a colleague. She says, "Forget solution number four. It's no good."

"Why?" you ask.

"Because it's a bad idea," she replies.

Your colleague has just committed a logical fallacy called *circular reasoning* (also known as *begging the question*). Circular reasoning is a very appropriate name, because that exactly what this logical fallacy does: It goes in a circle. Notice how your colleague's argument doubles back on itself. In other words, her argument (that the solution is "no good") and her support for that argument ("it's a bad idea") *say the same thing.*

Circular reasoning will most often hamper your problem-solving process by falsely justifying a decision to accept or reject a possible solution. If you say "no, that's not an effective solution" and can only explain why by saying "because it's no good," you're guilty of circular reasoning.

Here's another example. Vladimir chooses solution B over solutions A and C because, he says, solution B is the most economical, and cost was his number one priority when evaluating his solutions. However, when asked how solution B is most economical, Vladimir responds, "because it will cost the least." To justify his decision and avoid circular reasoning, Vladimir needs to show evidence that it is indeed the most economical (that it costs the least). A better response would be the following: "It's the most economical solution because it will cost a third of what solution A will cost and use half the resources that solution C would require."

NON SEQUITUR

Non sequitur is Latin for "it does not follow." It is an argument that makes a leap in logic. That is, it concludes B based on A, but there's not a logical connection between A and B. For example, let's return to the problem of having two reports due and not enough time to do them. Imagine that you decide the following:

> I can give one report to Pauline to do. After all, she helped me complete a report before; she can help me again.

Sounds good—except this is a non sequitur. Just because Pauline helped you before doesn't mean she'll be able to do it again. It's *possible* that she'll be available (and willing) to help you with a last-minute project, but you've made a jump in logic if you assume that it's true or *likely* to be true.

Here's another example. You're putting together a meeting schedule for your boss and come across a problem: The large conference room isn't available for a 2:00 meeting. You decide to schedule the meeting for the smaller conference room which is available. "After all," you reason, the "the last time she met with this company, only three people showed up. They won't need the large conference room."

This is clearly another non sequitur. Just because last time your boss met with this company only three people showed up, doesn't mean that this time there won't be ten people in the meeting. You've made an assumption, leaped from A to B, without checking to see that your conclusion was logical.

WORDS FROM THE WISE

"One cool judgment is worth a thousand hasty councils."
—*Woodrow Wilson*

Practice:

Do any of the following commit the logical fallacies discussed in this lesson: slippery slope, false dilemma, circular reasoning, or non sequitur?

1. Solution C is much better than solution D. It has more merit.
2. The supply room at the other office is kept under lock and key, so that's probably the best solution for this office, too.
3. Solution A is the best. It will take the least time to implement.
4. Don't waste your time brainstorming a solution. We only have two choices: to lock the supply room or have someone guard it.
5. If we install a video camera in the supply room, soon there'll be video cameras everywhere in the office. We'll be being watched all the time.

Answers:

1. Circular reasoning
2. Non sequitur. Just because it's the best solution for the other office doesn't mean it's the best solution for your office. It all depends upon how much the two offices and their employees are alike.
3. No logical fallacy
4. False dilemma
5. Slippery slope

In Short

The slippery slope fallacy assumes that if X happens, then Y will follow—but X isn't likely to lead to Y. A false dilemma poses only two choices when there are really many choices in between. Circular reasoning occurs when a statement and the support for that statement say the same thing. Finally, a non sequitur draws a faulty conclusion through a leap in logic by assuming that Y will happen just because X is the case.

Skill Building Until Next Time

1. Now that you are familiar with these logical fallacies, can you think of times when you've committed them?
2. Listen to how people justify their decisions. Do they commit any of these errors?

SECTION | V

IMPLEMENTING AND PRESENTING YOUR SOLUTION

Now that you've chosen the best solution for your problem, it's time to put your ideas into action. In this final section, you'll learn how to develop a detailed action plan for your solution. You'll also learn how to present your solution to others so that they clearly understand the problem and support your solution.

The last chapter in this book (Chapter 20) puts it all together for you by reviewing each of the steps in the problem-solving process and highlighting the key points of each chapter.

CHAPTER | 18

IMPLEMENTING YOUR SOLUTION

Once you've selected the best solution for your problem, it's time to put your ideas into action. This chapter explains how to create an action plan that will help you effectively implement your solution.

Do. Make. Spend. Cut. Order. Hire. Find. Determine. Create. Develop. Write. Explain. Visit. Show….

The list could go on and on. What all of these words have in common is that they are *action words* that you can use to make your solution a reality.

To effectively implement your solution, you need to turn your *ideas* into *actions.* That means you need to determine what actions are required to implement that solution, who will carry out those actions, how long those actions will take, how much they'll cost, and what you'll do if plans don't go as expected. In other words, you need to create an *action plan.*

WORDS FROM THE WISE

"A thought that does not result in action is nothing much, and an action that does not proceed from a thought is nothing at all."
—*Georges Bernanon*

CREATING AN ACTION PLAN

Creating an action plan—a plan to implement your solution—is the logical last step of the problem-solving process. There are six steps to creating an effective action plan:

1. Break the solution down into tasks to be accomplished.

2. Determine the order in which those tasks must be completed.

3. Determine who will handle each task.

4. Determine how long each task will take and how much it will cost.

5. Set specific start and end dates for each task.

6. Develop contingency plans.

Break Down the Tasks to Be Accomplished

In any solution, there are bound to be several, if not many, steps required to change the current situation to the desired situation. Begin drafting your action plan by listing each of the steps that must take place. Don't be afraid of breaking the steps down into small increments. For example, "Get voice-mail system" is actually a series of tasks that must be completed:

- Research voice-mail systems.

- Determine which is best for our needs.

- Shop for best price for that system.

- Get approval to purchase system.

- Purchase system.

So break the solution down into tasks, and break each of those tasks down if necessary. The more complete your breakdown, the more accurate and effective your action plan will be.

Practice:
Break the following solution down into tasks to be accomplished:

> *Let Renee know that I am uncomfortable with her gossip about colleagues.*

Answer:
Your answer will be unique, but it should look something like this:

- Decide when to talk to her.
- Decide where to talk to her.
- Decide what to say to her.
- Practice what to say to her.
- Decide how to say it to her.

Determine the Order in Which Tasks Must Be Completed

Obviously, if you're looking to get a new voice-mail system, you can't get approval for your purchase until you've determined which system to purchase. Just as you need to prioritize the questions to answer when you're researching your problem, you also need to prioritize the tasks to be accomplished when you create your action plan. Some tasks will need to be completed in order to make the completion of other tasks possible. Before you can begin assigning tasks, then, make sure they're organized in a time line that allows for steady progress.

Practice:
Organize the tasks from the previous Practice exercise in the order in which they must be completed.

Answer:

Your answer should look similar to the following:

1. Decide what to say to her.

2. Decide how to say it to her.

3. Decide where to talk to her.

4. Decide when to say it to her.

5. Practice what to say to her.

Determine Who Will Handle Each Task

Once you've determined the tasks and the order in which they need to be completed, it's time to determine who will handle each task. The next step will require you to assign values to each task, so at this point it makes good sense to create a chart that clearly lays out your action plan. Here's the complete chart; we'll talk about how to fill in all the blanks in a moment.

ACTION PLAN					
Task	Person	Time Frame	Cost	Start by	Finish by

To use this chart, fill in the tasks, in the order in which they must be completed, in the left-hand column. Then, assign the best person to each task. For example, if you have three tasks:

1. Conduct an inventory of the supply room.

2. Create an inventory database on the computer.

3. Write a memo to all employees about supply room policy.

You will probably assign each task to a different person who has the right expertise for the job.

Determine How Long Each Task Will Take and How Much It Will Cost

The next step is to determine how long each step of the solution will take. A half an hour? A day? A week? A month? Be as specific as possible, because the time frame will help you determine when to start and complete the task. Then, do the same for cost: Determine how much money you will need to invest for this particular part of the solution. If there is no other cost besides the employee's time, leave that column blank. Be sure to consider the cost of any supplies. For example, you might calculate the following for the tasks listed above:

ACTION PLAN					
Task	Person	Time Frame	Cost	Start by	Finish by
Conduct inventory	Amy P.	1 day	—		
Create database	Chad R.	1 week	$500 for soft-ware		
Write memo	Lou M.	3 hours	—		

Set Specific Start and End Dates for Each Task

In Chapter 3, we talked about the importance of having specific and measurable goals when you describe the desired situation. The same applies when you're implementing your solution. An action plan establishes specific goals for the implementation process: what task will be accomplished by when. So, on your chart, fill in a specific date for starting each task and a specific date for completing the task.

How do you determine when to begin a task and when it should be completed? Use your time frame and the order in which the tasks must be completed as your guides. Imagine, for example, that you have four tasks. The first three tasks must be completed before the fourth can begin. The first task will take one day; the second, three days; and the third, four hours. You have several options. You could start all three tasks on the same day and have a "finish by" date of three days from then, which is how long it will take to complete the longest task. Or you could start the longest task first, then bring in the second longest, and finally the shortest, so that they're all completed on the third day, as follows:

ACTION PLAN					
Task	Person	Time Frame	Cost	Start by	Finish by
1	AA	1 day		Tuesday	Wednesday
2	BB	3 days		Monday	Wednesday
3	CC	4 hours		Wednesday	Wednesday
4	DD	6 days		Thursday	next Friday

When calculating start and finish dates, it's important to keep in mind the other criteria for setting goals that we discussed in Chapter 3: Make sure your goals are ambitious and realistic. Certainly, if a task should take three days to complete, it's not realistic to start the task on Monday and expect to finish it by Tuesday. At the same time, you're not showing much ambition if you schedule to start a four-hour task on Monday and don't plan to complete it until Friday.

Practice:

Use the chart below to develop an action plan for your solution to the problem of not having enough money to make ends meet.

ACTION PLAN					
Task	Person	Time Frame	Cost	Start by	Finish by

Develop Contingency Plans

Once you have your action plan, you're all set to go, right? Well, not quite. You have your solution and a plan of action, and it's a good plan, but your plan depends upon everything working as expected. And that may not be the case.

To ensure the effectiveness of your solution, and to be sure to get support for your solution, it's important to develop contingency plans. Contingency plans are plans that are made *in case something happens.* In other words, they are back-up plans—plan B or plan C in case plan A doesn't work. These are all the more important if your solution depends upon outside factors, such as delivery of certain products or approval by certain individuals.

It'd be an awful lot of work if you developed contingency plans for each task in the action plan. In most situations, you will have a good idea which steps in the implementation process are most likely to run into roadblocks. For those steps, then, develop a plan B—and, if it's a particularly risky or shaky prospect, a plan C. For example, let's say you plan to talk to Renee about her gossiping. You plan to talk to her one morning in the cafeteria, as she's getting her morning cup of coffee, when she's not yet thinking about the day's work. However, the morning you're ready—after you've rehearsed what you want to say—she comes into the cafeteria later than usual, rushed, and in a bad mood. What do you do? Maybe you have plan B, which is to postpone until the time is right. But you might find excuses to put the talk off forever. A better plan B would be to tell her that you'd like to have a few minutes to talk to her later. Maybe she'd like to join you for lunch. That way you will still be able to implement your solution in the proper time frame. Even better, Renee will have some time to think about the reason you want to talk to her.

Practice:
Develop a contingency plan for at least one task in your action plan.

In Short

To effectively implement your solution, develop an action plan that:

- Breaks the solution down into specific tasks to accomplish
- Arranges those tasks in the order in which they must be accomplished
- Assigns a person to each task
- Specifies the time and cost to complete each task
- Specifies a start and end date for each task

Be sure to develop contingency plans as back-ups in case things don't go as you originally planned.

Skill Building Until Next Time

1. Action plans can be effective in many different situations, not just problem solving. Develop an action plan for something else in your life, like planning your vacation or hiring a new babysitter.

2. Consider your past experience with (or without) contingency plans. Have you ever gone ahead with an idea without thinking through any back-up plans? What happened as a result? Similarly, what situations have you "saved" because you had a contingency plan?

CHAPTER | 19

PRESENTING YOUR SOLUTION

You'll often have to present your solution to your colleagues or supervisors before you can begin to implement it. This chapter suggests several strategies for effectively presenting your solution.

Clarence had come up with the perfect solution for the company's shipping problem. He'd devised a new order processing procedure that cut out several steps and would get the product to the customer in just 6–10 business days. He drew up a detailed action. But the solution never got implemented. Why? Because Clarence didn't know how to present his solution to his colleagues.

While not officially part of the problem-solving process, presenting your solution to colleagues is essential to the success of your solution. This makes sense, since most problems and their solutions involve other people: Implementing a solution often requires the efforts of more than one person, and others will most likely be affected by changes resulting from your solution. And when you're solving problems at work, chances are you will need to get approval before you can implement a solution you've developed. But *how* you present that solution can determine whether or not the solution will be accepted by the powers that be.

Presentations may be formal or informal; you may present your solution to one person or to a hundred. Whatever the case, the same strategies apply. To effectively convince others that your solution is the most effective way to solve the problem, follow these five strategies:

1. Carefully consider your audience.

2. Clearly define the problem.

3. Summarize the problem.

4. Present the solution.

5. Anticipate objections.

CONSIDER YOUR AUDIENCE

The key to the success of *any* presentation is knowing your audience. What you say in your presentation depends entirely upon to whom you are saying it. In order to determine what to say, you need to answer the following questions about your audience:

1. **What do they know about the subject?** This will determine how much and what kind of information you will provide. Remember that you need to speak to the lowest common denominator. That is, if all of the people in your audience know A, some know B, and only a few know C, you have to speak on the level of A. If you speak on the level of B or C, you will lose some members of your audience—and that will make it difficult for them to support your solution.

2. **What preconceptions or misconceptions are they likely to have?** Are they likely to see the problem as a matter of poor management rather than inadequate computer technology? Are they assuming that the problem can only be fixed by hiring someone new?

3. **What experiences do they have in common?** Have they all been affected by the problem in the same way? Or have only some of them felt the effects of the problem? How will their experiences affect their acceptance of the solution? Imagine, for example, you are presenting a solution that requires everyone to learn new software. How many people are comfortable with computers? How will those who don't know much about computers feel about this solution?

4. **What perspective are they likely to have on the problem?** Are they looking at the problem from the point of view of the customer? The employee? Which employee? In other words, what relationship do they have to the problem?

5. **What solutions may they have come up with or be expecting for this problem?** Given their knowledge, pre/misconceptions, experiences, and perspectives, what solutions may they have thought of for the problem? What were the first solutions that came to your mind?

Answering each of these questions in detail will help guarantee an effective presentation. At a minimum, your audience will know that you've thought about them and their needs—and that counts for more than you think when you're trying to convince someone to accept your proposal.

CLEARLY DEFINE THE PROBLEM

As we discussed in Chapters 2 and 3, the first step in the problem-solving process is to clearly identify the problem. This is also the first step in presenting a solution, because what you're really doing for your audience is explaining your problem-solving process.

SUMMARIZE THE SCOPE OF THE PROBLEM AND THE KEY FACTS

As the person who has devised a solution, you've probably thought about the problem in more detail and, therefore, understand its scope more than those you're presenting to. You're also the one who researched the problem, so you understand better than the rest the facts of the case. You brainstormed solutions and selected the best one based upon those facts. Thus, if the people in your audience are to understand why the solution you chose is best, they need to know some of that background information. They need to know the scope of the problem (who does it affect? how? how long has it been going on? etc.) and they need to know the information you discovered as you researched the problem.

Imagine, for example, that you were presenting your solution to the shipping problem from Chapter 4. You decided that the best solution would be to completely revamp the order processing procedure because you learned, during your research, that the problem was in part caused by too many people handling the orders. Now imagine how your audience would react to that solution if they didn't know that eight different people dealt with an order before the product could be shipped. Chances are they would think your solution was unfounded, and perhaps even threatening. And they wouldn't support it.

WORDS FROM THE WISE

"No one is more definite about the solution than the one who doesn't understand the problem."
—*Robert Half*

PRESENT YOUR SOLUTION

Once you've provided the proper background by summarizing the scope of the problem and the key facts, it's time to present the solution. This actually includes three separate steps:

1. **Describe the solution.** Briefly describe how you plan to get from the current situation to the desired situation. What is your mechanism for change?

2. **Explain the evaluation and decision-making process.** How did you determine that this solution was better than the others? Describe other possible solutions and why they were rejected. Remember, some of the

members of your audience may have thought of similar solutions, so it's important to let them know why those ideas aren't as effective.

3. **Describe the implementation plan.** Show the audience that you not only have an effective solution, you have a detailed plan to put that solution into action. Seeing your action plan should convince your audience that your plan is logical, feasible, and effective.

ANTICIPATE OBJECTIONS

Often when you're trying to convince others to accept your point of view—that your solution is the best way to address the problem—your success will depend upon how well you are able to anticipate and address objections. Making accurate guesses about objections is easier when you've carefully considered your audience. When you address those concerns in a respectful, thoughtful way, you show your listeners that you really have thought carefully about the problem, that you've considered it from various perspectives besides your own, and that you are an open-minded and reasonable colleague.

Just how do you address those objectives, though, if no one has objected? Try a phrase like one of the following:

- It might seem like this solution is more expensive than we can afford. However, if you consider…

- "What about human resources?" you might be thinking. Well, that part of the problem is easy to address.

- Some of you might be thinking that this is going to lead to another problem with X. However, …

When addressing objections, you need to be careful not to inadvertently insult others who have thought of solutions that you have rejected. Choose your words carefully and avoid inappropriate responses like those listed in the chart below:

Some of you might have been thinking that the best way to approach this problem was X.

APPROPRIATE:	INAPPROPRIATE:
At first I thought so, too. However, when I learned that X … I realized that this solution would be too costly.	I thought so too. Boy was that a dumb idea. We'd go bankrupt if we tried to implement it.
And that solution makes a lot of sense. However…	Wrong! It costs too much.
Why not? After all, it's an easy, cost-effective solution. But…	Hope you didn't waste too much time thinking about that idea.

Practice:

Write an outline below for presenting the solution to your extra income problem to your spouse, your roommate, or someone else who is close to you and who will be affected by your solution.

In Short

How you present your solution can determine whether or not it will be implemented. Be sure to consider your audience, clearly define and summarize the problem, present your solution and action plan, and anticipate objections.

Skill Building Until Next Time

1. Consider presentations that you've given in the past. What made the successful presentations successful? What interfered with your success when the presentations weren't successful?

CHAPTER 20

PUTTING IT ALL TOGETHER: A FINAL REVIEW

This chapter will summarize the steps you learned in the problem-solving process and give you one last problem to solve, start to finish.

WORDS FROM THE WISE

"Nobody's problem is ideal. Nobody has things just as he would like them. The thing to do is to make a success with what material I have."
—*Frank Crane*

Congratulations! You've learned a great deal in this book, and before you put it back on the shelf, it's time for a quick review of what you've learned in each chapter. First, take a good look at the nine steps in the problem-solving process that you learned:

1. Identify the problem.

2. Determine its scope.

3. Research and summarize the problem.

4. Get in a creative mood.

5. Brainstorm for solutions.

6. Evaluate the solutions.

7. Select the best solution.

8. Create an action plan.

9. Present your solution.

Before you read the chapter reviews, are there any questions you have about these steps? Write them below. If the questions aren't answered in the review, take another look at that chapter to see if you can find the answer.

Questions:

Chapter Reviews

Chapter 1: A problem is an undesirable situation that is difficult to change. A solution is the mechanism for changing that situation. Problems are best expressed in a two-part problem statement that describes the current situation and asks a *how* question to express the desired goal.

Chapter 2: The statement that describes the current situation should be a fact, not an opinion. Facts are things *known* for certain to be true; opinions are things *believed* to be true. Problem statements must also avoid suggesting a solution and be focused enough to be manageable.

Chapter 3: A clearly articulated goal is essential for effective problem solving. A goal is something you are trying to reach or achieve. Your desired situation should be specific, measurable, ambitious, and realistic.

Chapter 4: Breaking the problem down into its parts enables you to determine the scope of the problem, making it more manageable. Determine the scope by asking *who, what, when, where, why*, and *how* questions about the current situation. Eliminate any questions that are irrelevant, and then group the questions into clusters of related issues. Next, prioritize those questions so that you can find answers quickly and efficiently.

Chapter 5: To effectively solve a problem, you need to know the facts and research its cause. Answer the questions you asked to determine the scope of the problem. As you research, keep accurate records, consider different levels of causation (multiple causes and chains of causation), and keep asking questions.

Chapter 6: The attitude you have towards problems can affect how successful you are in solving them. To have a positive attitude toward problem solving, face reality, embrace challenges, and trust your intuition. Know the environment in which you are most productive (consider lighting, furnishings, and background noise), and try to solve your problems in that kind of environment.

Chapter 7: Curiosity is essential to creativity and to effective problem solving. Cultivate your curiosity by being more observant. Ask questions about what you see. Try to think more like a child again.

Chapter 8: Successful problem solvers are able to see situations from various points of view or perspectives. They understand that different people see each situation differently because of their own unique background and experiences. Broaden your perspective by trying to see things from other people's points of view.

Chapter 9: Creativity is the ability to imagine or develop original ideas or things. We all have the ability to be creative, but some of us have let our "creativity muscles" go soft. Creativity helps us come up with powerful, effective solutions that others might not think of. Build your creativity by letting go of your fears. Stretch limits, make connections, see things in your mind's eye.

Chapter 10: We all suffer from "creativity block" from time to time. When you're having trouble coming up with an idea, re-start your creative energies by going for a walk, changing the scenery, looking to others for inspiration, or doing a creativity exercise like making up a dream.

Chapter 11: Brainstorming is the act of free-flow idea production. When you brainstorm, there is only one rule: anything goes. All ideas are valuable. Listing is a brainstorming technique that uses a free-flowing list to generate ideas.

Chapter 12: Two more brainstorming techniques are mapping and drawing connections. To map, put your desired situation in a circle in the middle of a blank piece of paper and brainstorm ideas. Put each idea in a circle and connect that circle to the idea that led you to it. To draw connections, select three random words and write freely about any connection those words have to your problem.

Chapter 13: A paradigm is a way of thinking about, perceiving, or understanding the world. Sometimes we get stuck thinking about problems because we are unable to think "out-of-the-box." Create a paradigm shift by changing an essential aspect of the problem that will force you to think about the problem in a new and creative way.

Chapter 14: To determine which solution is best, you can simply rank your possible solutions. But when the "best" solution depends upon what you mean by "best," you need to determine which criteria are important for your evaluation and then rank each solution according to those criteria. Common criteria include time, cost, feasibility, and risk.

Chapter 15: Another way to evaluate solutions is to list the pros and cons for each possible solution. Because some pros and cons will carry more weight than others, your evaluation will be most effective if you assign a value (1–10) for each pro and con.

Chapter 16: Even when we carefully evaluate solutions, we often choose the wrong one because we make a mistake in reasoning, like giving in to appeals to emotion. We might choose the wrong solution because we feel flattered, scared, or sorry for someone, or because we want to belong.

Chapter 17: Slippery slope is another common mistake in reasoning. It assumes that if X happens, then Y will follow—but there's not a strong causal relationship between X and Y. A false dilemma is when we assume there are only two possible choices. Circular reasoning is an argument that goes in a circle (you say the same thing twice in two different ways), and a *non sequitur* is a leap in logic that assumes Y will happen just because X exists.

Chapter 18: Once you've selected the best solution, develop an action plan to put your ideas into action. Your action plan should break the solution down into various tasks that need to be accomplished and arrange those tasks in the order in which they should be accomplished. Then, assign a person to complete each task. Determine how long each task will take and how much it will cost. Finally, determine a specific start and end date. Don't forget to develop contingency (back-up) plans in case things go wrong.

Chapter 19: To effectively present your solution and get others' support for your idea, be sure to carefully consider your audience—who they are, what they know, and what they expect or want to hear. Clearly define the problem, summarize its scope and the key facts, and present your solution. Be sure to include a description of your evaluation and decision-making processes. Then, describe your implementation plan. Don't forget to anticipate objections.

Practice:

One last problem for you to solve. We've given you the current situation. Your goal is to find a good solution. Your first step will be to determine the desired situation.

> **Current situation**: One of your colleagues, with whom you are good friends, has applied for the same promotion that you are after. You are competing against each other for the same position.

Whatever solution you came up with for this problem, if you followed the nine steps in the problem-solving process and avoided common errors in reasoning, it's bound to be a good one!

Remember that the more you use the steps in this process, the more quickly you will develop your problem-solving skills. Before you know it, the process will become second nature, and you'll be able to address problems of all kinds with confidence and ease.

Remember, too, that successful problem solving depends upon the right attitude towards problems and on keeping a problem-solving disposition. So, keep stimulating your curiosity, keep cultivating your creativity; and always remember—not all opportunities are problems, but all problems are opportunities for you to succeed.

 ## WORDS FROM THE WISE

"The difficulties and struggles of today are but the price we must pay for the accomplishments and victories of tomorrow."
—*William J. H. Boetcker*

Skill Building Until Next Time

Congratulate yourself for addressing a problem (your ability to deal with problems) and successfully implementing your solution (completing this book)!

APPENDIX

ADDITIONAL RESOURCES

- Bierman, Arthur K., and R. N. Assali. *The Critical Thinking Handbook.* Prentice Hall, 1995.
- Bransford, John D. *The Ideal Problem Solver: A Guide for Improving Thinking, Learning, and Creativity.* W H Freeman & Co., 1993.
- Browne, M. Neil, and Stuart M. Keeley. *Asking the Right Questions: A Guide to Critical Thinking.* Prentice Hall, 1997.
- Burns, Marilyn. *50 Problem Solving Lessons.* Marilyn Burns Education Assoc., 1996.
- Burns, Marilyn. *The Book of Think: Or, How to Solve a Problem Twice Your Size.* Demco Media, 1976.
- Dawson, Roger. *The Confident Decision Maker: How to Make the Right Business and Personal Decisions Every Time.* Quill, 1995.
- Diestler, Sherry. *Becoming a Critical Thinker: A User-Friendly Manual.* Prentice Hall, 1997.
- Edwards, Ronald. *Problem Solving Through Critical Thinking.* Addison-Wesley, 1993.

- Fearnside, W. Ward. *About Thinking*. Prentice Hall, 1996.
- Fobes, Richard. *The Creative Problem Solver's Toolbox: A Complete Course in the Art of Creating Solutions to Problems of Any Kind*. Solutions Through Innovation, 1993.
- Fogler, H. Scott, and Steven E. Leblanc. *Strategies for Creative Problem Solving*. Prentice Hall, 1994.
- Freeley, Austin J. *Argumentation and Debate: Critical Thinking for Reasoned Decision Making*. Wadsworth, 1997.
- Higgins, James M., et al. *101 Creative Problem Solving Techniques: The Handbook of New Ideas for Business*. New Management Publishing Co., 1994.
- Hunter, Dale, et al. *Co-Operacy: A New Way of Being at Work*. Fisher Books, 1998.
- Jones, Morgan D. *The Thinker's Toolkit: Fourteen Powerful Techniques for Problem Solving*. Times Books, 1998.
- Kaye, Harvey. *Decision Power: How to Make Successful Decisions With Confidence*. Prentice Hall, 1992.
- Kennedy, Debbie. *Breakthrough! The Problem-Solving Advantage: Everything You Need to Start a Solution Revolution*. Leadership Solutions Publishing, 1998.
- Kidder, Rushworth M. *How Good People Make Tough Choices*. William Morrow & Company, 1995.
- Levine, Marvin J. *Effective Problem Solving*. Prentice Hall, 1994.
- Little, Linda W., and Ingrid Greenberg. *Problem Solving: Critical Thinking and Communication Skills*. Addison-Wesley Publishing Co., 1991.
- Lumsdaine, Edward and Monika. *Creative Problem Solving: Thinking Skills for a Changing World*. McGraw Hill, 1994.
- MacKall, Dandi Daley. *Problem-Solving (Career Skills Library)*. Ferguson Publishing, 1997.
- Marten, Mary and Marty. *Problem Solving*. Western Horseman, 1998.
- Mayer, Richard E. *Thinking, Problem Solving, Cognition*. W H Freeman & Co., 1992.
- Missimer, C.A. *Good Arguments: An Introduction to Critical Thinking*. Prentice Hall, 1994.

- Moore, Brooke Noel, and Richard Parker. *Critical Thinking*. Mayfield, 1998.
- Murphy, Jim. *Managing Conflict at Work*. Irwin Professional Publishing, 1993.
- Noone, Donald. *Creative Problem Solving: Barrons Business Success Guide*. Barrons Educational Series, 1998.
- Paustian, Anthony. *Imagine! Enhancing Your Problem-Solving and Critical Thinking Skills*. Prentice Hall, 1996.
- Romain, Dianne. *Thinking Things Through: Critical Thinking for Decisions We Can Live With*. Mayfield, 1996.
- Roth, William. *Problem Solving for Results*. Saint Lucie Press, 1996.
- Stevens, Michael. *How to Be a Better...Problem Solver*. Kogan Page, 1997.
- Thomas, David A., and Maridell Fryar. *Successful Problem Solving*. National Textbook Co., 1997.
- Turner, Thomas. *Brainstorms: Creative Problem Solving*. Scott Foresman & Co., 1991.
- Van Fleet, James K. *Lifetime Guide to Success With People: Instant Solutions to Your Toughest Problems—On the Job, in the Community, With Family and Friends*. Prentice Hall, 1995.
- Watzlawick, Paul, et al. *Change: Principles of Problem Formation and Problem Resolution*. W W Norton & Company, 1988.
- Weiss, Donald. *Creative Problem Solving (Successful Office Skills)*. AMACOM, 1988.
- Wycoff, Joyce. *Mindmapping: Your Personal Guide to Exploring Creativity and Problem-Solving*. Berkley Publishing Group, 1991.
- Yep, Dorothy S. *Creativity at Work (Business Skills Express)*. Irwin Professional Publishing, 1994.

Order Form

CALIFORNIA EXAMS
___ @ $35.00   CA Allied Health
___ @ $35.00   CA Corrections Officer
___ @ $35.00   CA Firefighter
___ @ $20.00   CA Law Enforcement Career Guide
___ @ $35.00   CA Police Officer
___ @ $30.00   CA Postal Worker
___ @ $34.95   CA Real Estate Sales Exam
___ @ $35.00   CA State Police
___ @ $18.95   CBEST (California Basic Educational Skills Test)

NEW JERSEY EXAMS
___ @ $35.00   NJ Allied Health
___ @ $35.00   NJ Corrections Officer
___ @ $35.00   NJ Firefighter
___ @ $20.00   NJ Law Enforcement Career Guide
___ @ $35.00   NJ Police Officer
___ @ $30.00   NJ Postal Worker

TEXAS EXAMS
___ @ $18.95   TASP (Texas Academic Skills Program)
___ @ $32.50   TX Allied Health
___ @ $35.00   TX Corrections Officer
___ @ $35.00   TX Firefighter
___ @ $20.00   TX Law Enforcement Career Guide
___ @ $35.00   TX Police Officer
___ @ $30.00   TX Postal Worker
___ @ $29.95   TX Real Estate Sales Exam
___ @ $30.00   TX State Police

NEW YORK EXAMS
___ @ $15.95   CUNY Skills Assessment Test
___ @ $30.00   New York City Firefighter
___ @ $25.00   NYC Police Officer
___ @ $35.00   NY Allied Health
___ @ $35.00   NY Corrections Officer
___ @ $35.00   NY Firefighter
___ @ $20.00   NY Law Enforcement Career Guide
___ @ $30.00   NY Postal Worker
___ @ $35.00   NY State Police

MASSACHUSETTS EXAMS
___ @ $30.00   MA Allied Health
___ @ $30.00   MA Police Officer
___ @ $30.00   MA State Police Exam

ILLINOIS EXAMS
___ @ $25.00   Chicago Police Officer
___ @ $25.00   Illinois Allied Health

FLORIDA EXAMS
___ @ $32.50   FL Allied Health
___ @ $35.00   FL Corrections Officer
___ @ $20.00   FL Law Enforcement Career Guide
___ @ $35.00   FL Police Officer
___ @ $30.00   FL Postal Worker

REGIONAL EXAMS
___ @ $29.95   AMP Real Estate Sales Exam
___ @ $29.95   ASI Real Estate Sales Exam
___ @ $30.00   Midwest Police Officer Exam
___ @ $30.00   Midwest Firefighter Exam
___ @ $18.95   PPST (Praxis 1)
___ @ $29.95   PSI Real Estate Sales Exam
___ @ $25.00   The South Police Officer Exam
___ @ $25.00   The South Firefighter Exam

NATIONAL EDITIONS
___ @ $20.00   Allied Health Entrance Exams
___ @ $14.95   ASVAB (Armed Services Vocational Aptitude Battery): Complete Preparation Guide
___ @ $12.95   ASVAB Core Review
___ @ $19.95   Border Patrol Exam
___ @ $12.95   Bus Operator Exam
___ @ $14.95   Catholic High School Entrance Exams
___ @ $14.95   Federal Clerical Exam
___ @ $14.95   Pass the U.S. Citizenship Exam
___ @ $14.95   Police Officer Exam
___ @ $12.95   Postal Worker Exam
___ @ $12.95   Sanitation Worker Exam
___ @ $18.95   Treasury Enforcement Agent Exam

NATIONAL CERTIFICATION & LICENSING EXAMS
___ @ $20.00   Cosmetology Licensing Exam
___ @ $20.00   EMT-Basic Certification Exam
___ @ $20.00   Home Health Aide Certification Exam
___ @ $20.00   Nursing Assistant Certification Exam
___ @ $20.00   Paramedic Licensing Exam

CAREER STARTERS
___ @ $14.95   Administrative Assistant/Secretary
___ @ $14.00   Civil Service
___ @ $14.95   Computer Technician
___ @ $14.95   Cosmetology
___ @ $14.95   Culinary Arts
___ @ $14.95   EMT
___ @ $14.95   Firefighter
___ @ $14.95   Health Care
___ @ $14.95   Law Enforcement
___ @ $14.95   Paralegal
___ @ $14.95   Real Estate
___ @ $14.95   Retailing
___ @ $14.95   Teacher
___ @ $14.95   Webmaster

To Order, Call TOLL-FREE: 1-888-551-JOBS, Dept. A040

Or, mail this order form with your check or money order* to:

LearningExpress, Dept. A040, 20 Academy Street, Norwalk, CT 06850

Please allow at least 2-4 weeks for delivery. Prices subject to change without notice   **NY, CT, & MD residents add appropriate sales tax*

 LEARNINGEXPRESS®

NOTES